T0278723

WE NEED TO
TALK ABOUT
Xi

**WHAT WE NEED TO KNOW
ABOUT THE WORLD'S
MOST POWERFUL LEADER**

MICHAEL DILLON

EBURY
PRESS

Ebury Press, an imprint of Ebury Publishing
20 Vauxhall Bridge Road
London SW1V 2SA

Ebury Press is part of the Penguin Random House group of companies
whose addresses can be found at global.penguinrandomhouse.com

Penguin
Random House
UK

First published by Ebury Press in 2024

www.penguin.co.uk

A CIP catalogue record for this book is available from the British Library

ISBN 9781529914450

Typeset in 12/15.5pt Bell MT Std by Jouve (UK), Milton Keynes
Printed and bound in Great Britain by Clays Ltd, Elcograf S.p.A.

The authorised representative in the EEA is Penguin Random House Ireland,
Morrison Chambers, 32 Nassau Street, Dublin D02 YH68

MIX
Paper | Supporting
responsible forestry
FSC® C018179

Penguin Random House is committed to a
sustainable future for our business, our readers
and our planet. This book is made from Forest
Stewardship Council® certified paper.

Contents

Xi's Timeline

1949	People's Republic of China established
1953	Xi Jinping is born on 15 June
1958	Mao Zedong's Great Leap Forward
1959–61	Widespread famine resulting in at least 20 million deaths
1966	Mao's Cultural Revolution
1974	Xi Jinping joins Communist Party
1975	Xi Jinping enrols at Tsinghua University to study chemical engineering
1976	Mao Zedong dies
1978	Xi Zhongxun (Xi's father) rehabilitated
1979	Xi Jinping graduates; appointed secretary to Geng Biao in Ministry of Defence
1982	Xi working in Zhengding village, Hubei
1983	Deng Xiaoping takes power
1985	Xi visits United States of America; appointed deputy mayor in Xiamen, Fujian
1987	Xi and Peng Liyuan marry
1988	Xi moves to Ningde in Fujian as party secretary

People and Places

Chinese surnames normally come before given names. Some Chinese people, especially when living outside China, reverse this to fit in with Western usage. Some also have Western given names.

Bo Xilai – Chongqing party secretary who introduced anticorruption drive and Red Culture campaign. Convicted of corruption and imprisoned for life in 2013.

Chen Liangyu – Shanghai party secretary, removed from office in 2006 over pension scandal. Xi Jinping succeeded him.

Chen Min'er – Contender for party general secretaryship in 2022. Remains in Politburo.

Chiang Kai-shek – Guomindang nationalist president of China until 1949 on the mainland and in Taiwan until his death in 1975.

Fang Lizhi – Astrophysicist and democracy campaigner.

Geng Biao – Minister of defence and Xi Jinping's first employer and mentor.

Gu Kailai – Wife of Bo Xilai, imprisoned for life in 2012 for the murder of a British businessman.

He Guoqiang – Head of Chinese Communist Party (CCP) Central Organisation Department and Central Commission for Discipline Inspection. Key supporter of Xi in People's Republic of China (PRC) bureaucracy.

He Lifeng – Economist and vice premier in Xi administration with responsibility for banking and other financial regulators.

Hu Chunhua – Contender for CCP general secretaryship in 2022. Excluded from Politburo.

Hu Jintao – CCP general secretary from 2002 to 2012.

Hu Yaobang – CCP chairman and general secretary from 1981 to 1987.

Jiang Qing – Wife of Mao Zedong, leader of the Gang of Four, and Mao's would-be successor.

Jiang Zemin – CCP general secretary from 1989 to 2002.

Ke Hua – Chinese ambassador to the UK and the father of Ke Lingling.

Ke Lingling – Xi Jinping's first wife.

Lam, Carrie (Carrie Lam Cheng Yuet-ngor) – Hong Kong chief executive until 2022.

Lee Ka-chiu, John – Senior police officer and Hong Kong chief executive from 2022.

Li Keqiang – Premier in the first decade of Xi administration.

Li Qiang – Shanghai party secretary and premier in Xi's extended administration from March 2023.

Liu He – Economist and vice premier in Xi administration.

Liu Shaoqi – PRC chairman (president) from 1959 to 1968 and opponent of Mao Zedong's Cultural Revolution.

Mao Zedong – Chairman of the CCP till his death in 1976.

Peng Liyuan – Popular singer, People's Liberation Army officer, and Xi Jinping's second wife.

Sun Yat-sen – First president of Republic of China in 1912 and revered by both CCP and nationalist Guomindang (GMD) as the founding father of modern China.

Tsai Ing-wen – President of Taiwan 2016 to present day.

Tsinghua University – Elite university in Beijing and alma mater of many senior Chinese politicians.

Wen Jiabao – Premier in Hu Jintao administration.

Xi Heping – Xi Jinping's half-sister who died during Cultural Revolution.

Xi Mingze – Xi Jinping's daughter.

Xi Zhongxun – Xi Jinping's father.

Zhongnanhai – 'Central and Southern Lakes', the HQ of the CCP – China's Kremlin.

Zhou Enlai – Respected premier and foreign minister under Mao Zedong 1954 to 1976.

Introduction: Why We Need To Talk About Xi

ON 23 OCTOBER 2022, Xi Jinping greeted the press in Beijing's Great Hall of the People, strutting well ahead of his Politburo Standing Committee colleagues. In the well-cut business suit that is de rigueur for senior Chinese officials on such formal occasions, he appeared fresh and overflowing with confidence as he emerged from the full session of the 20th National Congress of the Chinese Communist Party. It had just accorded him an unprecedented, but not surprising, third term as general secretary of the party for an additional five years.

Fast forward to Sunday 5 March 2023, when the National People's Congress, the nearest thing China has to a parliament, opened in Beijing. It is typically dismissed as a 'rubber stamp parliament', which is not entirely inaccurate, but it is nevertheless an important event. It is an opportunity for several thousand movers and shakers from around the country to confer and intrigue in person, and it allows the leadership to demonstrate who is really in power. Xi demonstrated his personal authority with great confidence – some might say arrogance and complacency – when on Friday 10 March he was awarded an extension of the presidency and the chairmanship of the government side of the Central Military Commission. This confirmed his occupancy of the three great offices of the Chinese state; his chairmanship of the Chinese Communist Party element of the Central Military Commission had already been confirmed by the party.

Who is Xi Jinping? What makes him tick? He has often been portrayed in the Western press as a power-hungry dictator and tyrant. Is he just like his Russian counterpart, Vladimir Putin? What effect is he having on China today? And what does this mean for the future – not only for China, but for all of us? In the following chapters, I hope to answer these questions and give as accurate a picture as possible of the most powerful leader in the world.

In order to understand Xi Jinping, we need to look at the history that created him. This is not just because I am a historian, but because the historical background is essential for understanding what is happening today. Xi Jinping, and indeed the whole of the Chinese Communist Party (CCP), often think and speak in historical terms. Many of the issues in which Xi has been involved are complicated because of their history. This is made more complex because the CCP's interpretation of history does not always overlap with Western academic narratives. Much of it does, but a great deal of the CCP version is deeply nationalistic and operates on assumptions about what can or should be included in the territory of China, Taiwan being an obvious example.

China is at a historic turning point. For decades, it has been opening up to the wider world and modernising its economy under its successive leaders: Deng Xiaoping, Jiang Zemin and Hu Jintao. Xi Jinping appears determined to reverse much of this process and recreate China in his own image. Will the rest of the CCP leadership accept this, or will he be more constrained by opposing factions during his extended period in office? After all, his reselection was for five years only, not the ten that had previously been the rule. This is the core question facing China and the world today. But to really understand it, and to understand Xi Jinping himself, we have to turn the clock back a few decades to the world in which Xi Jinping grew up and learned to be a politician.

When I began to study Chinese seriously in the late 1960s, China was a closed book. The Cultural Revolution was at its height and Westerners were not welcome to visit. It was unquestionably Mao's China, although there were other powerful leaders and Mao Zedong did not always get his own way. Images of thousands of young, militant Red Guards massing in Tiananmen Square in the summer of 1966, as Chairman Mao donned their distinctive armband to their frenzied adulation, stunned and horrified observers. This was not the solid and staid communism of the Soviet Union. What did it mean?

As I and my fellow students were struggling to understand the significance of *Quotations from Chairman Mao Tse-tung* – the Little Red Book – and wrestling with the bizarre and often violent vocabulary of the Cultural Revolution, Xi Jinping was one of hundreds of thousands of young Chinese sent to the countryside to live and work with the peasants.

Much later, we were able to see that behind the revolutionary rhetoric and marching teenagers lay a brutal struggle for power: Mao was ailing and his rivals were battling to succeed him. When Mao died in September 1976, for many Chinese this seemed like the end of the world. They had known no other leader, and many feared what might happen next. The previous July, the city of Tangshan, to the northeast of Beijing, had been hit by a devastating earthquake that caused up to 250,000 deaths. For some, this was an omen: it heightened the atmosphere of panic and a dread that some mysterious cosmic changes were taking place. After a period of chaos, Deng Xiaoping, an opponent of Mao's radical policies, was brought back to Beijing from internal exile by premier Zhou Enlai to bring order out of the chaos.

Deng's 'reform and opening' policies were the basis for the spectacular rise of China, opening it up as Mikhail Gorbachev did with the Soviet Union. Throughout this time, unlike in the former Soviet Union, the CCP remained in power; there was no room for multiparty democracy, in spite of pressures from some activists. This was the world in which Xi Jinping had matured personally and politically. After years of chaos and political infighting, the Deng Xiaoping period offered a new order of stability and astonishing growth. The Communist Party had remained in control but by the late 1980s it was a different party with different priorities.

The 1980s saw the birth of the democracy movement, particularly in Beijing. There had always been dissenters, both within and outside the Communist Party. The younger generation were frustrated by bureaucratic restrictions, limited career options, corruption, inflation and the inequality that I had observed during my travels. Opening to the outside world had increased awareness of demands for democracy in Eastern Europe and elsewhere. Manifestos

and political essays calling for greater democracy
were posted on Democracy Wall, a wall on what is
now one of the central shopping streets in Beijing,
Xidan Road. Hu Yaobang, the party leader who was
sympathetic to these demands, was ousted in 1987,
but demonstrations in Tiananmen Square grew in
size and intensity. Zhao Ziyang, who succeeded Hu
and attempted to negotiate with the demonstrating
students and citizens, was himself purged and what
had been a permanent democracy camp in Tiananmen Square was destroyed in a military assault on 4
June 1989. This cost the lives of hundreds, possibly
thousands, of demonstrators and wrecked the democracy movement, but it also deeply scarred the
army and the Communist Party, of which Xi was a
member. The People's Liberation Army (PLA) had
attacked the people, as dissenters noted; this was not
the kind of battle of honour that regiments of the
PLA relished. The decision to crush the demonstra-
tion was opposed by many in the Party and that
created lasting divisions. The democracy movement
did not survive the 4 June killings and they served
as a warning to Xi Jinping's generation of the risks
inherent in pressing for democracy.

Following the Tiananmen Square massacre,
Jiang Zemin was brought in as a safe pair of hands.
During his term as party leader, from 1989 to 2002,

foreign observers began to question whether China was still a 'communist' state. The party had withdrawn from day-to-day involvement in the economy and had invited businessmen to become members. Foreign firms were beginning to operate in China in a way that had hardly been possible since 1949. China continued to open up to foreign travellers. This level of access to distant parts of China continued when Hu Jintao came to power in 2002. Hu and his lively and vociferous premier, Wen Jiabao, were enthusiastic about continuing Deng Xiaoping's reform and opening policies. Wen Jiabao in particular encouraged people to criticise bureaucratic malpractices.

The ability to travel freely and independently, and not as a member of an organised or official group, was invaluable in assessing how the lives of people in China were changing. So was the opportunity to work with students at Tsinghua University in Beijing, one of the top two universities in the country, as a visiting professor in 2009. Being in the heart of Beijing with inquisitive students was a great privilege. They were not cut off from the outside world: the book barrows that turned up outside the campus every evening brought cheap paperbacks both in Chinese and English, and this included works by American novelists such as John Grisham and Michael Connelly, which were snapped up by eager students as well as foreign academics. Conversations over coffee and lunch at the café attached to the top local academic bookshop enabled me to keep up to date with the political gossip, which included discussions about whether Bo Xilai would become premier. He didn't – but at the time his wife had not yet been found guilty of murdering a British businessman and Bo had not yet been imprisoned for embezzlement.

In 2010, I was able to carry out an extended programme of fieldwork in Xinjiang, mostly in the southern cities of Kashgar and Khotan. I was able to walk around Kashgar uninterrupted, photographed the destruction of the old city and the intimidating patrols of heavily armed police and military units in what was a stronghold of anti-Chinese sentiment. I stayed overnight on a farm run by the Xinjiang Production Construction Corps, much feared for its role in putting down demonstrations by Uyghurs.

China after Mao was far from perfect – any demands for multiparty democracy were put down firmly and dissidents had been imprisoned or exiled. For most Chinese people, however, life was more tolerable than before the reforms. Many were prepared to accept 'economic democracy' (decent jobs or the ability to make money) at the expense of 'political democracy'. It was a trade-off, and it was better than it had been under Mao. In the early years of Xi Jinping's administration, it looked as if his rule was going to be much the same. However, as he consolidated his control everything began to change.

Chapter 1: One-man Triumvirate

He is determined to become this man who saves
the party and the nation . . . he needs to grab
power in the party, government, military, police
and ideology to rejuvenate the country.
*Chen Daoyin, Shanghai University of Political Science
and Law, Voice of America, March 2023*

HOW HAS XI JINPING got himself into a position where
he is being compared with Chairman Mao? Many
informed commentators would argue that he is the
most powerful Chinese leader since Mao. What has
Xi done differently from his predecessors to justify
this claim? To answer these questions, we need to
dig deeper into the political structure of the People's
Republic of China (PRC). Xi's impressive-sounding
titles are president of China, general secretary of
the Chinese Communist Party and chairman of the
Central Military Commission. These are the three
great offices of the Chinese state, but what do
they mean?

Xi Jinping is often referred to as President Xi, the first of these offices. This is correct, but somewhat misleading as it obscures the real basis of his power. In China the president is called the state chairman (国家主席, *guojia zhuxi*) but official translations have used the term 'president' since 1982 to demonstrate equivalence with foreign heads of state. This position is symbolic and principally ceremonial, but it is essential for China to play its proper role in international diplomacy.

The more important position, and the second great office, is the leadership of the Chinese Communist Party (CCP). The head of the CCP is currently referred to as general secretary. This title was used in the early days of the party but Mao, when he was party leader, was always Chairman Mao: between 1949 and 1959 he was both party chairman and state chairman. CCP leaders since Mao have rejected the title of party chairman to distance themselves from him. Since 1981, the official position of the CCP has been that Chairman Mao made major mistakes in his leadership of the country, mainly the Great Leap Forward in 1958 and the Cultural Revolution from 1966. He cannot be airbrushed completely out of the history of the PRC as he was clearly the most powerful of the founding fathers. In spite of this official ruling, there are still

individuals and groups in China who run websites
to show that they support all of Mao's policies. In
general, the adulation of Mao and the cult of the
personality associated with his rule have been a
source of considerable embarrassment for today's
CCP. Loyal party members have written many
books and articles critical of Mao; for example, Yang
Jisheng's books *Tombstone* and *The World Turned
Upside Down*. Even Xi Jinping, who emulates aspects
of Mao's style of ruling, has not insisted on being
called chairman of the Communist Party. Addressing
the Politburo Standing Committee (a small group –
currently seven of the top leaders of the CCP and
including the general secretary) in November 2012
after his election, he simply said, 'We have just held
the First Plenary Session of the 18th CCP Central
Committee and elected a new central leadership. I
was elected general secretary of the Central Committee.' This was unanimous as is invariably the case
and there was no suggestion that he should be called
Chairman Xi.

The third of these great offices is chairman of
the Central Military Commission, which grants
control over all of China's armed forces. Whoever
holds that office is effectively commander-in-chief of
the land, air and naval units of the PLA. Theoreti-
cally, there are two Central Military Commissions,

the second being a government rather than a party body, but that is really a technicality; their memberships are identical and they meet as one body.

Xi Jinping has been appointed to all three positions – a one-man triumvirate – as have his predecessors, but it is the title of general secretary of the Chinese Communist Party that really matters. Indeed, it is the only position of the three that Mao held continuously until his death. That is where power really lies in contemporary China; the authority of the military commission and the presidency derive from the party. In Deng Xiaoping's day, the term 'paramount leader' was widely used to indicate Deng's extraordinary authority and his control of the three great offices of the Chinese state. This was never a formal Chinese title, although there is a Chinese equivalent (最高领袖 *zuigao lingxiu*), which simply means 'highest leader'. Deng exercised his authority while remaining personally modest.

Below these posts and the Communist Party apparatus that supports them sits the Chinese government, a gargantuan bureaucratic machine with ministries and departments like any other state, although given the size of China, it is on a much grander scale. It operates at central, provincial and lower levels, and at its head is the premier (总理 *zongli*), sometimes called prime minister, and four

security. These are directly responsible to Xi and therefore carry higher authority than other party bodies and the entire apparatus of the government. Xi has used them to drive through his policies against any opposition and to enhance his own power and prestige within the party and the country. Xi Jinping's immediate predecessors did not have this level of authority and the equivalent under Mao was the Cultural Revolution Group, which divided the party and ushered in the chaos of the Cultural Revolution. Xi has learned not to follow that route.

Can we say precisely what system was used to produce leaders of China in Mao's declining years and immediately after his death? The simple answer is that there was no system at all. Leaders emerged out of discussions or, as Chinese colleagues have frequently and vehemently reminded me, 'struggles' (斗争 *douzheng*) within the party, with the winner being whoever emerges on top. There is some level of internal democracy, and voting in the selection of key party posts increased during the Hu Jintao period, but it was really a question of who could impose their will by rhetoric, threat or inducement. Mao was able to impose his will through his stature as revolutionary leader as well as his force of personality. Bluntly speaking, people were afraid of him. Xi does not have revolutionary credentials and

must rely on the force of his personality and his political wiles.

Mao Zedong was chairman of the Chinese Communist Party until the end of his life in September 1976, but after 1959 he was no longer state chairman (president). He had to step back from that role, which was largely ceremonial, after the dreadful failure of the Great Leap Forward and the famine in its aftermath in which tens of millions of people, mainly in the rural areas, died. Mao had rivals for power. The most important and the best known was Liu Shaoqi, who took over from him as state chairman in 1959. The rivalry between Liu Shaoqi and Mao Zedong was one of the main triggers for the Cultural Revolution, which threw China into turmoil for roughly a decade between 1966 and Mao's death in 1976. The memory of the Cultural Revolution may have faded but it has not vanished: most contemporary Chinese political leaders have been determined to avoid a repetition, but Xi Jinping's actions suggest that he is more equivocal. In *The Governance of China*, 500 pages of his speeches, Xi Jinping only mentions the Cultural Revolution twice, although his profile in the appendix declares that he 'suffered public humiliation and hunger, experienced homelessness and was even held in custody on one occasion'. If that is all, he got off lightly

compared with many political leaders and their families.

As Mao aged and his physical and mental health declined, a vicious struggle for succession broke out among the senior leadership of the Chinese Communist Party. Mao's wife, Jiang Qing, was seen as a possible new chairman, although she was personally unpopular. Jiang Qing had led the ultraradical faction in Shanghai that toppled the local party apparatus during the Cultural Revolution. In her younger days, in the 1930s, she had been an actress in the city's burgeoning film industry and married Mao Zedong in 1938. This was against the wishes of his CCP colleagues: she was seen as a political liability, and she had also supplanted his previous wife who had been a loyal communist and followed him on the Long March. Jiang and her colleagues were blamed for much of the violence of the Cultural Revolution, in some cases unfairly, and there is no doubt that misogyny played a part in her unpopularity. She was known as a bully who used extraordinarily bizarre language and had a violent temper. This was deployed in her extended feud with the popular premier, Zhou Enlai, who had been attempting to bring some order to the increasingly irrational chairman's rule for many years, but with limited success. In the hysterical and overheated language of the Cultural Revolution, Jiang Qing was dubbed 'lady white-bone demon' and feared and ridiculed in equal measure. Driving past her former residence in Shanghai in 1986, my Chinese colleagues pointed out the house in which she had lived in hushed tones.

Jiang Qing clearly believed that she was the rightful inheritor of Mao's mantle but so did Lin Biao, the minister of defence and a senior and successful Marshal of the People's Liberation Army. Lin Biao's fate was sealed in 1971 when his planned coup against Mao was uncovered and he attempted to escape, possibly to the Soviet Union, even though it had recently been at war with China. The aircraft in which he was travelling, a British-built Trident, crashed in Mongolia killing him, his family and his entourage. Mao's widow and her key supporters, now known as the Gang of Four, were put on trial for treason and imprisoned in 1981. It had been a chaotic period for the leadership of China and Deng Xiaoping, an opponent of Mao's radical policies, was brought back to Beijing from internal exile by Premier Zhou Enlai in 1973 to bring order out of the chaos.

Vice Premier Deng Xiaoping had worked with President Liu Shaoqi and Premier Zhou Enlai for years attempting to mitigate Mao's irrational policies. This earned him exile from Beijing during the Cultural Revolution, which he spent in a tractor

factory in the southern province of Jiangxi. Eschew-
ing the title of chairman, Deng introduced his
famous 'reform and opening' (改革开放 *gaige kaifang*)
policies. The most important aspects of these were
the withdrawal of the Chinese Communist Party
from the direct management of economic enterprises and avoiding a repetition of the Mao years
where one leader could determine so much of China's policy. Deng prioritised growth over ideology,
reduced the involvement of the Communist Party in
the day-to-day management of the economy, and
encouraged the development of special economic
zones as pilot studies for market-oriented projects.
Deng was convinced that for China to move forward
it must never again have one single dictatorial leader.
He included himself in that and did not rule in a dictatorial way. It is precisely these aspects of the
reforms that Xi Jinping has attempted to reverse.

The 1980s in China were a period of confusion,
but also of intellectual ferment. China under Deng
Xiaoping had been offered the 'four modernisations'
of agriculture, industry, defence, and science and
technology. Many argued that there should be a fifth
modernisation: democracy. This all came to a bloody
end on 4 June 1989; images of the tanks rolling into
Tiananmen Square still appear on posters of human
rights organisations.

Jiang Zemin was brought in from Shanghai as general secretary of the Chinese Communist Party to replace the leadership that had been compromised over the crushing of the democracy movement. Jiang was not well known nationally but, as party leader in Shanghai, he had managed to engage with the democracy movement without causing any bloodshed.

By this time ideas for a new system of selecting the leader, and indeed the whole leadership, of the Communist Party was beginning to emerge under the influence of Deng Xiaoping, the reformist deputy premier under Zhou Enlai who was purged by Mao during the Cultural Revolution. The fundamental idea was that the general secretary of the party, who would also take the other two great offices, would be selected for two five-year terms. The successor would be chosen halfway through the ten years, would serve under that leader for the second five-year term as a deputy, and would then take over for his own (or her – but that is probably wishful thinking) full ten-year term. Under this system, no one leader could hold the position of general secretary in perpetuity. The overlap would assure continuity as new leaders emerged.

The first general secretary to be chosen under the new system was Hu Jintao in 2002 and Xi Jinping himself benefited from the system when he was elected in 2012, after having been appointed deputy in 2007 halfway through Hu Jintao's administration. It was widely assumed that this new system would carry on more or less permanently and that Xi would serve five years as deputy to Hu Jintao, follow with his own administration of ten years and that halfway through that decade, a successor would be chosen to take over from him at the end.

Nothing that was publicly known about Xi Jinping at the time of his appointment in 2012 led anyone to believe that he intended anything different, but it became gradually apparent that he was much more comfortable with the idea of a single individual leading China than with the more collective and collegial system that had been developed under Hu Jintao. Rumours began to spread about his authoritarianism, as his policies (which we'll explore in more detail in the following chapters) were distinctively different from those of his predecessor, Hu Jintao. He failed to allow the emergence of a successor halfway through his ten-year term of office and began his manoeuvres to extend the term of president that was limited by the constitution of the PRC – there was no constitutional limit in the case of the other two great offices. It became obvious that he aspired to stay in power for much longer than the conventional ten years and people began speaking of him as 'president for life'.

Not surprisingly, opposition grew within the upper echelons of the Communist Party, although that opposition was rarely made public. The strict enforcement of the CCP's principles of democratic centralism, and not openly criticising whoever was chosen as leader, were deeply ingrained. Xi finally managed to achieve his aim in the autumn of 2022 when he succeeded in persuading the National Congress of the Communist Party to give him the extra five years, which he had been insisting on for a long time. He had effectively overturned the system that had brought him to power in 2012. The immediate effect of this extension was to block prominent rivals for the post of general secretary, such as Chen Min'er and Hu Chunhua, but the impact is more far reaching. The ten-year system had enabled officials to plan their careers at all levels of the Chinese party and government bureaucracy. By overturning the system, he has thwarted the ambitions of thousands of cadres who were expecting preferment under the new general secretary, particularly those who had been associated with Hu Jintao and the Youth League faction of the party. Although he has emerged from the party conference and the NPC with his desired extension, he has also created resentment and potential resistance to his policies.

Chapter 2: Princeling Outsider

An ostracised princeling's ascent to the top
Straits Times, *October 2022*

ONE OF THE SECRETS of Xi Jinping's rise to power has been his ability to stand aside from, and transcend, the factional struggles within the Chinese Communist Party. The CCP goes to great lengths to disguise dissent or even any serious difference of opinion within its ranks. This is because of its adherence to the principle of democratic centralism. In theory, all political issues are thrashed out in private and, when an agreement is reached, no party member is permitted to indicate any dissent. There is no provision for minority opinions, which are effectively suppressed; there is only the official policy. Where a European equivalent might permit a minority report or an individual might resign on a point of principle, the Chinese (and indeed the Soviet) rule was that there could be no deviation from the official, and therefore the correct, policy. This is rigorously enforced in

China and disagreement in public with party policy can be treated as treachery.

This does not mean there are no factions. In a party that now has a membership of well over 96 million, drawn from widely differing parts of China, social backgrounds and even ethnic groups, how could there not be? However, it is extremely difficult to pin them down. They cannot operate as factions with open meetings, manifestos and slates of candidates as has become commonplace in multiparty democracies. So, attempting to determine who is in what faction, and which are gaining influence or losing support at any particular time, is highly problematic. Political factions in China are based on allegiance to an individual leader or a group of people associated with a particular city or province, rather than to an ideology or policy. The best known example is the Shanghai faction, which became powerful under the administration of Jiang Zemin and earned notoriety when its members tried to exercise authority after Jiang had stepped down as general secretary.

There is almost no acknowledgement in official CCP publications that these factions exist, although they are known to all Chinese people who take any interest in their own politics. In addition to the Shanghai faction, which was gaining power within the party in the 1990s, there is another prominent group known as the Youth League faction. The Chinese Communist Youth League is the junior branch of the CCP and the organisation that people normally join first if they have an ambition to become full members of the party later. The Youth League tends to attract bright, ambitious students and other young people who maintain and develop their league membership, and subsequently party membership, as they progress through their careers. Xi Jinping, like most party members, joined the Youth League before he became a CCP member in 1974 but he did not work his way up through the league's bureaucracy, so he was never a member of the Youth League faction.

Members are drawn from the alumni of the huge Youth League bureaucracy, which has its own newspaper, among other publications, and runs regular meetings and training sessions. Although most, if not all, CCP members were in the Youth League, it is those who served in its central offices who have continued their closest political association. The Youth League faction had an important role in Xi Jinping's rise because among its key members are Hu Jintao, Xi Jinping's immediate predecessor as general secretary of the Communist Party, and Li Keqiang, who served as premier under

Xi Jinping. Li Keqiang was almost certainly side-lined by Xi Jinping because of his association with the Youth League faction, which Xi Jinping has come to oppose and despise. It is not obvious why, but it is probably connected with Hu's collective leadership style and tolerance of foreign influences. Others associated with the faction were Hu Yaobang and Hu Chunhua.

The term 'princelings' is often used in discussions around the Communist Party. 'Princelings' is the usual common translation of 太子党 *taizi dang*, which literally means the 'party of the crown princes' and refers to the sons and daughters, nieces and nephews or other close junior relatives of senior leaders of the Communist Party.

Princelings have often been treated as a faction by political scientists, but, in reality, they are just a mutual support group exercising patronage. Bo Zhiyue, a political scientist at the Victoria University of Wellington in New Zealand, has shown how this group can be subdivided according to the background of their families. These included military and political families but also those from a more entrepreneurial background, such as the state-owned financial and industrial conglomerate CITIC (China International Trust Investment Corporation), and those who had married into princeling families.

Princelings are children of senior party officials who
went to school with each other, associate with each
other socially and protect each other's families and
careers. As the diverse backgrounds indicate, their
interests were far from identical. It would be natural
for them to enter the Communist Party and move
swiftly up through its ranks. Given the nature of
Zhongnanhai (中南海), the party and government
complex in the centre of Beijing, many of them will
be living in close proximity to each other. These
princelings have no distinctive political coherence
and no bureaucratic organisation, in contrast to the
Youth League, which has a legitimate bureaucratic
organisation as a subsidiary or junior part of the
Chinese Communist Party. Because of this lack of
institutional organisation, it is impossible for them
to operate as a group or to exercise any collective
political power. What they can do, and do as a matter
of course, is exercise widespread influence by the
well-known Chinese concept of connections (关系
guanxi). Connections are of course important any-
where but the idea of *guanxi* has particular resonance
in Chinese society. The quality and weight of the
princelings' *guanxi* is much higher than most of the
rest of the population of China can wield, and this has
led to nepotism on a grand scale and the ability of
some 'princelings' to amass fortunes in business as

China privatised major sectors of the economy. There is a parallel here with the emergence of the oligarchs in post-Soviet Russia but in China these assets have not gone primarily to the security apparatus.

One thing that really distinguishes Xi Jinping is that he does not associate himself, at least publicly, with the princelings. In fact, many argue that he deliberately avoids being categorised as a princeling. Although he is under no illusions about his own background, and how other people categorise him, he rejects any discussion about what he calls the 'stars in the political firmament' (政坛明星 *zhengtan mingxing*), the powerful people in the party and government elite with whom he might have connections. Those connections are very real but Xi has so far avoided the severe criticism of nepotism made of other senior officials of the Hu Jintao period. He might be a 'princeling', but he is also an outsider with no faction of his own who has outmanoeuvred the other factions.

Born in 1953, Xi was educated at the exclusive August 1st School, named after Army Day, which educates the children of CCP leaders from primary to high school level at three campuses a few miles north of the Zhongnanhai party compound. Zhongnanhai was where the most powerful families lived and worked. The school nurtures the attitude that

its pupils have an innate right to leadership, not dissimilar to that found in Britain's Eton College and
similar elite schools in the West. Those students
who were born into revolutionary families, (自来红
zilaihong), are even said to disdain the rest as mere
'staff' (伙计 huoji). Like most of his generation, Xi's
education was interrupted by the Cultural Revolution. How it affected him personally is not entirely
clear: although he was not old enough to be a Red
Guard, he was seized by various Red Guard groups
and obliged to denounce his father, a common
experience of the children of high officials. His half-
sister Xi Heping is said to have committed suicide
under the pressure of Red Guard intimidation.

Xi Jinping's high-level connections begin with
his father Xi Zhongxun, who was born in 1913 and
died in 2002, the year in which Hu Jintao, the most
senior figure in the Youth League faction, came to
power as general secretary of the Chinese Communist Party. Xi Zhongxun was a well-known and highly
respected guerrilla leader in the 1930s, leading one
of the important guerrilla forces against the invad-
ing Japanese army. On the basis of his military
record and his party membership, he rose through
the party ranks and eventually became a member of
the CCP Politburo and Secretariat. On the government side, he became Secretary General of the State

Council, a position subsidiary to the Premier which equates roughly with that of cabinet secretary in Western democratic governments. Xi's mother Qi Xin was born in 1926 and lives in Beijing. She was a veteran revolutionary, educated in colleges run by the CCP, and actively supported Xi's father when he was persecuted. She worked in the Communist Party School but later concentrated on her family. Xi is said to be close to his mother and was strongly influenced by her simple and frugal lifestyle and the warm but strict family atmosphere that she created. She was alert to the dangers of corruption. According to a semiofficial biographical account, 'After Xi Jinping became a leading official, his mother called a family meeting to ban the siblings from engaging in any business in the areas where Xi Jinping worked.' Xi, in turn, threatened to deal with them ruthlessly if they did not comply.

Xi Zhongxun's career progressed well in the 1950s, but in 1962 he was purged on the orders of Mao Zedong for something extremely trivial that probably tells us more about Mao Zedong than it does about Xi Zhongxun: he was dismissed simply because he supported the publication of a fictionalised account of a guerrilla leader, which Mao felt diminished his own role in guerrilla warfare.

In 1966, before Xi Zhongxun could be rehabilitated, the Cultural Revolution erupted and like many
other bureaucrats and moderates within the Chinese
Communist Party he was persecuted for several
years, sent down to the countryside, put in charge of
a tractor factory at one point and spent some time in
prison or under house arrest. He was not formally
rehabilitated until 1978, the second year after the
death of Mao Zedong, but he returned to important
posts within the party, mainly in Guangdong province, the economic powerhouse in southern China.

He held the most senior posts in Guangdong,
the province that led China's economic transformation, and was an enthusiastic supporter of economic
liberalisation. However, during Deng's 'reform and
opening' years in the 1980s, Xi Zhongxun seems to
have put himself on the wrong side of political history by being a defender of the moderate CCP
general secretary Hu Yaobang, who was himself
purged in 1987. Soon enough, Xi Zhongxun found
himself picked out, disgraced, and pushed out of
office by the party's ruling group. He became isolated and he had little support from his colleagues
after the purging of Hu Yaobang. Xi Jinping has not
been publicly forthcoming about his attitude towards
his father's career but the fact that he isolated

himself from so many of the senior party leadership and their families suggests that he blames them for his father's political disgrace.

Xi Zhongxun was reputed to be tolerant and evenhanded, more like Deng Xiaoping or Zhou Enlai than Mao Zedong. In areas that he governed in the 1950s, he rejected the most draconian forms of repression and managed to reduce the number of individuals executed for 'counter-revolutionary activities' by 50 per cent. He also encouraged direct elections for new government bodies and banned physical punishments and unnecessary attacks on landlords. When Xi Jinping was about to become CCP general secretary, there were great hopes that he would emulate his father's more liberal and reformist approach.

The Cultural Revolution is conventionally dated as having taken place between 1966 and 1976, although it came to an end earlier than that in some parts of China and its effects continued long afterwards in the whole country. During the Cultural Revolution, Xi Jinping was sent down to the countryside, like so many other young people of his age: his official profile in *The Governance of China* says that he 'volunteered' but it is unlikely that he had any real choice. This 'rustication' (下放 *xiafang*) or 'sending down' programme, as it became known, was partly an ideological matter. It was considered vital to educate what some of the party believed to be a generation of pampered urban youths to appreciate the hardships of peasant life when they became adults and began to develop their careers, and it was believed that there was something natural and genuine about peasant life that would purify those brought up in shady and immoral urban settings. The Chinese Communist Party had come to power primarily on the back of peasant organisation and peasant armies: veteran peasant activists were often sceptical about urbanites and especially educated young city people. Rustication was also a necessary strategy. As the Cultural Revolution began to fizzle out, the new leadership that emerged felt the need to defuse the Red Guard movement that had spread through China at Mao Zedong's instigation and was threatening to get out of control.

Xi Jinping was sent to the village of Liangjiahe in northern Shaanxi, a poor and relatively isolated area in the northwest of China, and one of the areas that had been an important part of the Communist Party's rise and its resistance to the Japanese invasion forces. It was also, perhaps not coincidentally, close to his father's hometown. The young Xi spent around four years in northern Shaanxi on farms, working hard on tough agricultural work, which he described in various autobiographical notes, including this from Xia Fei's *Taizidang he gongqingtuan* (Princelings and Communist Youth League), published by Hong Kong Mirror Books in 2007.

> For a whole year I did not rest at all unless I was actually ill. In rain and wind I chopped up hay for fodder in a cave with [the peasants] and at night I watched over the animals. I took the sheep out to pasture and did all kinds of jobs and at that time I would carry 200 *jin* (100 kilo) of wheat on my shoulders for 10 *li* (5 kilometres) along a mountain road without shifting it from one shoulder to the other.

The countryside of northern Shaanxi is stunning but rugged. Much of the farming is on terraced hillsides as there is little flat land. My own experience of these 'mountain roads' in west and central China is that they are often little more than steep tracks, perhaps marked with rudimentary stone steps in dangerous places and tough to climb, even without a load of grain. There is no doubt that Xi genuinely experienced the life of millions of peasant farmers who often have to walk for miles on these tracks to get essential supplies from neighbouring villages.

During this period, he was living in what were little more than huts or sheds, getting up early as all farmers do, and spending his days doing backbreaking manual labour. He formed close relations with some of the peasant families with whom he worked and lived, but they were only too aware of his privileged background. Later in life, when he became a senior political figure, he was able to repay some of the kindness that they had shown him by offering to pay for medical expenses and other commodities and services that the poor families in northern Shaanxi could not afford. While he was on the farm, he was to some extent protected by this privileged background; local people, especially people in the rural Communist Party branches, knew that young Xi was somebody with connections and might be useful or important in the future. It would be a good idea to look after him. He admits that he was completely unable to cook for himself, so one of the villagers would prepare meals for him while he did what he was really interested in – reading and studying, which impressed his neighbours. This was solid preparation for his later academic career and his eventual doctorate in law from Tsinghua University. The cave in which he lived has been turned into a tourist attraction – almost a shrine – and is a magnet for Chinese people who want to see for themselves

where President Xi was sent down to the countryside in the Cultural Revolution.

During his sojourn in the countryside in 1974,
he joined the Chinese Communist Party, although
his application is said to have been rejected several
times. This was not unusual, but in his case it may
have been connected with his father's political disgrace. Xi Jinping became the party secretary of his
local village branch in northern Shaanxi; it would
not of course disadvantage the local Communist
Party to have as their branch secretary someone who
was so well connected. As the Cultural Revolution
drew to a close, he managed to get a place at Tsinghua University to study chemical engineering.

Tsinghua University is one of the top two universities in China – the correct pinyin spelling for
its name 清华 is *Qinghua*, but the university prefers
the older version. Its rival is Beijing University, but
Tsinghua claims to have produced more senior leaders who were willing to undertake the 'double
burden' of political leadership and high-level technical knowledge required for China's economic and
technological development. I was a visiting professor at Tsinghua in 2009, long after Xi had left, but
its role as a leadership university was still obvious.
Although the atmosphere during the Hu Jintao
period was generally relaxed, there were still strict

taboos, as I discovered when I blundered by mentioning Xinjiang during a talk on China's relations with Pakistan.

Xi Jinping was enrolled in this elite university, but the irony is that he was accepted because he was able to qualify as a member of what was known at the time as the 'worker–peasant–soldier' category. In theory, this was intended to discriminate in favour of students from poor but politically active backgrounds. Xi Jinping could technically be regarded as a peasant on the basis of his years of rustication.

Chapter 3: Cautious Climb to Supreme Power

An unremarkable provincial administrator.
Evan Osnos, New Yorker, *March 2015*

XI ENTERED TSINGHUA AT a turbulent time for China's universities: they were in the throes of a concentrated effort to rebuild their faculty and student bodies after having been effectively closed down for at least eight years during the Cultural Revolution. If his acceptance by Tsinghua was an indication of the advantages of a privileged background, his first job after leaving the university was even more so – and it is in this period of his life that the political leanings of young Xi were being formed by the people, problems and viewpoints he encountered.

Even though he was a raw graduate, his first posting was to the Central Military Commission, the body that oversees the management of the entire People's Liberation Army. By the spring of 2013 he would be chairman of that commission, although in 1979, even the young Xi Jinping brimming with self-confidence could hardly have imagined that this would be part of his future role. He became secretary to Geng Biao, already at that time a Politburo member and later minister of defence, whose office, like almost all the most powerful departments, was in Zhongnanhai, the party and government complex in the centre of Beijing. Zhongnanhai has evolved into a closed and secretive community where the most senior officials live and work. Xi Jinping had moved directly from his poor rural environment in Shaanxi into Beijing's equivalent to Moscow's Kremlin. He only remained in that environment briefly: Geng Biao advised him to avoid a purely military career if he wanted to get on in life, and before Geng's death in June 2000 at the age of 90, he was able to see the results of his advice.

Xi's first appointment marked him out as someone with exemplary social and political connections (关系 *guanxi*) but, after leaving the Ministry of Defence in 1982, he followed a career path that thousands of Chinese government and party officials had already taken, moving through the provinces, circling around and gradually approaching the top tiers of the ruling elite in Beijing. This well-worn path had been trodden not only by Chinese Communist Party cadres but for centuries before them by officials serving the Chinese Empire that eventually collapsed in 1911.

The type of party and government posts that Xi took show how his experiences affected his outlook. It is not always clear whether he chose these appointments or whether he was directed to them, but this was the path he had to follow if he wanted to succeed in politics, which he clearly did. The nature of the Chinese bureaucracy is such that he could only be appointed when appropriate positions became vacant and his first posting outside Beijing was as deputy party secretary in Zhengding County in Hebei province. Hebei is a sprawling north China region of mixed industry, mining and agriculture, which more or less surrounds Beijing. Zhengding, a traditional village in Zhengding County with a distinguished tradition of Chan (Zen) Buddhism, is about 150 miles south of Beijing.

Xi stayed in Zhengding for two or three years and in 1985 moved to Fujian, which was well on its way to becoming one of China's wealthiest provinces thanks to the country's modern economic transformation. Fujian lies on China's south-eastern coast and faces Taiwan directly. It has its own distinctive culture and local people are proud of their distinctive Fujian languages; usually called Hokkien throughout Asia, they are not readily comprehensible to speakers of Mandarin or Cantonese. The southern version, Minnan, is also called Taiwanese when it is spoken on the island of Taiwan and the linguistic connection has greatly facilitated business links between Taiwan and the mainland. Fujian is well known for its entrepreneurialism and for emigrants who have made their fortunes in Southeast Asia and elsewhere in the Asia Pacific region.

All in all, Xi Jinping spent a total of 17 years in Fujian province, beginning as deputy mayor of the great port city of Xiamen (historically called Amoy by Westerners). In 1990, after relatively smooth progress through the party and government bureaucracies, he became party secretary of the city of Fuzhou, the administrative capital of Fujian province. This was a prestigious and powerful appointment, the party secretary being senior to the governor who ran the local government. Xi was moved from Fujian province in 2002 to become party secretary in neighbouring Zhejiang province, another rapidly developing province of the southeast that was well known for its great banking families and for being the home province of Chiang Kai-shek, the nationalist leader and great opponent of the Chinese Communist Party. Migrants from the city of Wenzhou in Zhejiang are in the majority in overseas Chinese communities of the Netherlands, Italy and Spain. Traders from Wenzhou have also operated throughout China and they own and run what are commonly called Wenzhou hotels (温州旅社 *Wenzhou lüshe*) which provide cheap accommodation for travellers, probably the most basic I have ever encountered in China.

It was at this point that Xi Jinping also became a member of the Communist Party Central Committee. This is the powerful CCP body that currently has 205 full members and 171 alternates. It is the body that formally chooses the even more powerful Politburo and the general secretary; joining its ranks is a significant step for aspiring Chinese politicians. Xi was building himself a reputation as a tireless worker and he spent a great deal of time on what is usually known in Chinese as inspection visits, travelling round his bailiwick and visiting outlying villages. He made a point of going to the poorest and most remote areas and became very well known for his industry and frugality. In a pun that works rather better in Chinese than it does in English, he was known as 'two planks' (两板 *liangban*): the boss (老板 *laoban*) during the day, but sleeping on a hard wooden bed (地板 *diban*) at night. In other words, although he had high rank and great authority, he was keen not to exploit his status by showing the trappings of power. This style of leadership, which draws on a tradition of heroic officials in Chinese history and literature, was particularly significant in his attitude towards corruption in the party and government, which will be examined more closely in chapter 5.

Xi's Zhejiang posting was important because that province had become a model for the economic development of China. Ironically, in view of some of the things that he was later to do as general secretary, Xi Jinping is credited with developing the private sector in Zhejiang. He was pushing at an open door as Zhejiang already had a history of entrepreneurism and flourishing private businesses. He was also a great advocate for the integration of the economies of the separate provinces of the Yangtze Delta region and this wider perspective would prove important for his political future.

On a personal level, Fujian was important to Xi Jinping because it was there that he met his second wife, Peng Liyuan. He had previously been married to Ke Lingling, the daughter of diplomat Ke Hua who was appointed ambassador to the United Kingdom in 1978 and was deeply involved in negotiations over the handover of Hong Kong. That marriage had broken down in 1982, possibly in part because of Xi's rural posting, although insiders claim that they quarrelled all the time. Ke Lingling travelled to Britain to be with her father – she may still be in the UK. Xi's marriage to Peng Liyuan has apparently been much more successful and they have one daughter, Xi Mingze, who has studied at Harvard.

Like almost all CCP leaders, Xi is fanatically reticent about his private life, but there are glimpses in some official publications, including a profile at the end of Xi's book, *The Governance of China* (2014) – clearly designed to enforce the image of Xi as the perfect husband as well as the perfect leader. It describes how when Peng was on tour, 'Xi would phone her before bedtime almost every night, no matter how late it was.' It goes on to say, 'In the eyes of Peng, Xi is a good husband and a good father. She always shows care and consideration for him. Peng takes every opportunity to be together with her husband, cooking dishes of different styles for him. To Peng, Xi is both a unique and an ordinary person . . . He likes swimming, mountaineering, and watching basketball, football and boxing matches.' Image is all important for Xi and nothing but praise would be allowed in a book like this.

When Xi and Peng married in 1986, Peng Liyuan was far more famous than him. She was well known as a singer of traditional folk songs, as a soprano in Chinese operas including *The White Haired Girl* and *Ode to Heroine Mulan,* and had appeared frequently on television. She is also a member of the People's Liberation Army because she sang with various military choirs and bands, often touring in the more remote areas of the country. She sometimes appeared in military uniform and is said to have had a military equivalent rank of major general – far outranking Xi Jinping. Both her popularity as a singer and her military connections were useful for Xi Jinping, who had no real military background. When Xi was appointed deputy chair of the Central Military Commission in 2008, there was an unexplained delay; some insiders claimed that there had been resistance to Xi's appointment and that it was his marriage to Peng that finally swayed the doubters.

By this time, it was becoming clear to many that Xi Jinping was destined for greater things. It was assumed that his next move would be a promotion to a position in the central government or the party centre, which would have taken him back to Beijing. This did not happen. In September 2006 there was a crisis in Shanghai. The party secretary, Chen Liangyu, a member of the Politburo and part of the powerful Shanghai faction of the party, was dismissed. He was accused of having misused pension funds and in 2008 was convicted of bribery, stock manipulation and financial fraud, and sentenced to 18 years' imprisonment. Xi Jinping replaced him as party secretary of Shanghai in 2007.

Although Xi Jinping had worked with Shanghai people and had taken an interest in the development of Shanghai, he had never been a member of, or even closely associated with, the Shanghai faction, which had been the dominant faction during Jiang Zemin's term of office as CCP general secretary. At that time, there were really only two powerful factions within the Chinese Communist Party: the Shanghai faction and the Youth League (or Communist Youth League) faction. The Shanghai faction was in decline and, in the eyes of many CCP members, the Youth League faction had become arrogant, overbearing and unpopular. Xi Jinping moved into Shanghai as an outsider but with connections to Shanghai and its economy.

He also came armed with a reputation for being deeply opposed to corruption and strongly in favour of reforming official institutions and practices. 'Worms can only grow in something rotten,' he informed the Politburo as he railed against the corruption that he saw 'raging' through the party. A speech he made to the Central Commission for Discipline Inspection, the party's internal equivalent of the KGB or the Gestapo, was called 'Power Must Be Caged by the System', referring to the caging of the 'tigers' of corruption as well as the 'flies'. In another speech to the same body, he quoted from the poem 'Keep Your Hands out of

Other People's Pockets' written by the respected PLA commander and politician, Chen Yi: 'Do not try dipping into the public coffers because a thieving hand is bound to be caught.' Party members do not like to talk about corruption or how it is investigated, but some have made it clear to me how much the internal security agents are feared.

At this time, Xi Jinping was being supported by key figures within the inner circles of the Communist Party, notably He Guoqiang who was director of the Central Organisation Department, one of the powerful but usually invisible departments that actually runs the Communist Party. He Guoqiang had earmarked Xi Jinping not only for the Shanghai post, but for higher office. So, it is not surprising that in October 2007, at the 17th Congress of the Communist Party, Xi Jinping was elected to the Politburo Standing Committee, a group of between five to seven people selected from the decision-making body the Politburo. Operating at this very high level within the party meant that Xi Jinping could no longer stay in Shanghai. He had to demonstrate that he had progressed from being a regional leader to one focused on the government of the whole country. After moving with his wife and family to Beijing, he worked and lived within the party centre, the key move that put him in line for the top position.

At this point it is worth stepping back to look at what support Xi had and the influences that he brought into the elite levels of the Communist Party. Some of this influence can be traced back to the career of Xi Jinping's father, Xi Zhongxun, who had been deeply respected by Hu Yaobang, the reform-minded former general secretary who was ousted in 1987 for being *too* reform-minded. Hu Yaobang had supported Xi's immediate predecessor, Hu Jintao, and was therefore an early representative of what became the Youth League faction. Because Hu Yaobang respected Xi Zhongxun, he also became committed to supporting Xi Jinping, although he never gave his formal 'imperial endorsement' to Xi Jinping's nomination for the highest office. This imperial endorsement is today used for the recommendation of a successor by a political leader. The reference to the bureaucratic processes of the empire is ironic considering these processes are oblique to anyone not in the system, but also revealing as many similarities to this old process remain.

Hu Jintao, following his mentor, Hu Yaobang, supported Xi Jinping at this point. Xi Jinping was not associated with Hu Jintao's Youth League faction, but neither was he associated with the rival Shanghai faction. One crucial act of Hu Jintao, which indirectly and unintentionally helped Xi Jinping on his way to becoming general secretary, was Hu's insistence on increasing internal democracy within the Communist Party. In practice, this meant extending the voting system so that senior positions had to be elected. It is another of the unusual phenomena of the Hu Jintao administration that information about these voting systems became more widely available. They had been known about generally for years but not in the detail that found its way into the press in the early 2000s.

It is likely that this new more open system for selecting leaders helped Xi Jinping's advancement. Nevertheless, it is clear that Xi was personally popular because of his reputation as an effective and honest provincial leader. The Central Organisation Department that was supporting Xi Jinping circulated a questionnaire among non-party members in the National People's Congress and the Chinese Political Consultative Conference, which indicated overwhelming support for Xi. Why was there this level of support? Simply put, he was regarded as a classic 'virtuous official', to use a term that was common for centuries throughout Chinese imperial history. He had a clean record and was not corrupt. As the Chinese economy had expanded, the opportunities for corruption at all levels had increased and there was a growing revulsion in China against corrupt officials, particularly those at the very top who were being accused of handling bribes and kickbacks amounting to millions of *renminbi* and imprisoned.

This was all well and good but, looking at it from Xi Jinping's point of view, there was a serious problem. The list of people who had supported him over the years included his father, Xi Zhongxun, who was purged in 1962; Hu Yaobang, a great supporter of both Hu Jintao and Xi Jinping, purged in 1987; and Zhao Ziyang, who was Hu Yaobang's open-minded successor, purged in 1989. All had been champions of increased democracy and openness within the Communist Party. All, one way or another, lost their power and their jobs. They were forced out by the more authoritarian and illiberal elements of the party.

This discouraging legacy was not lost on Xi Jinping. In 2007, there were interesting reports that he knew he was being considered for the highest offices but was unwilling to climb to the top. It is difficult to verify these reports but, if they are true, was it a case of genuine unwillingness, was it false modesty, or was it a cunning tactic to get power by any means? Was he acutely aware that if he were to come to power and behaved like his father and other more open-minded colleagues, he would be in danger of being overthrown in the same way?

In any case, Xi Jinping began to stand out as the only possible candidate as a successor to Hu Jintao. He was not without his critics: colleagues in Zhejiang described him as simple and honest to a fault, which was not intended as a compliment – the implication was that he didn't have the capacity to deal with complex problems. As the Chinese economy and Chinese society were developing, the problems that would confront a general secretary were becoming increasingly complicated. Xi was not charismatic, but that could be seen as an advantage since many Chinese were wary of charismatic politicians after their experience with Mao Zedong and his abrasive and arrogant manner. By contrast, Xi's management style, at least when he was working his way up the ladder, was seen as consensual: he did not offend people unnecessarily and he formed good working relationships – although this does not appear to have continued once he achieved high office. He was seen as a safe pair of hands. He might not have had any spectacular successes in the provinces where he had served, but there had been no real disasters either and he had arrived in Beijing armed with a track record of fostering successful economic developments. There were great hopes for a new era of progress but what transpired was not what most people inside or outside China expected.

Chapter 4: Authoritarian Despot or China Dreamer?

Preservation of the Party comes before preservation of law.
Evan Osnos, New Yorker, *March 2015*

XI JINPING HAS BEEN criticised for being unusually authoritarian and his ruling style is often described as a 'new authoritarianism'. This is hardly surprising after the increased use of mass surveillance, crackdowns on internet and other tech companies, and his role in repressing opposition and dissent in Hong Kong and Xinjiang. But let us get one thing straight: China has *never* had any form of democracy. The political structure we see today is the product of centuries of rule by authoritarian despots – imperial, nationalist and communist. So, is Xi really that different from the leaders that have gone before?

The official ideology of the Chinese Communist Party, when it came to power in 1949 and inaugurated the People's Republic of China, was Marxism-Leninism-Mao Zedong Thought. In other words, it was an attempt to follow the ideological guidelines set by the Soviet Union, adding what were claimed to be important contributions made by Mao. There is no agreement, even among Marxists, about how important these contributions of Mao really were, but for members of the CCP what was significant was that these were Chinese contributions. Mao was Sinifying Marxism: creating a unique philosophy that was appropriate to the conditions of China and advanced the theory of Marxism. He and his supporters claimed this as a more appropriate ideology for China and an improvement on the Soviet model, which in Mao's view was guilty of backsliding.

This Marxism-Leninism-Mao Zedong Thought, which became known as Maoism, lasted as the official ideology, without being seriously challenged in the CCP, until the Cultural Revolution broke out in 1966. This threw China into political chaos on a grand scale and much of the bureaucratic management of the country fell into abeyance. Maoism turned into the unthinking adulation of Mao Zedong and Mao Zedong Thought. *Quotations from Chairman Mao Tse-Tung* – a list of political aphorisms, drawn from the speeches and articles in his *Selected Works* – better known in the West as the Little Red Book, was required reading. It was brandished and

quoted by all and sundry but particularly by juvenile
Red Guards, the teenage shock troops of Mao's Cultural Revolution, many of them of secondary-school
age who formed independent pro-Mao groups and
roamed the country demonstrating their adulation
of Mao. The political chaos undermined belief in official ideology. Rational supporters of Mao struggled
to force his 'thoughts' into a consistent ideological
structure, while slogans and demonstrations replaced
management and reason. Enthusiasm for the upheaval
began to peter out in 1968 and 1969. The People's
Liberation Army took control to oversee the creation of a new CCP structure and government, and
the unruly Red Guards were sent down to work in
the countryside before being allowed back to school
or college.

During the 1960s and 1970s, foreign political
scientists, government analysts and many others
spent thousands of precious hours attempting to
understand the thinking behind Mao's writings and
speeches, and predict the direction in which China's
policy was going to go. Similar hours were spent
on the verbose and frequently incomprehensible
outpourings of Red Guard organisations, whose
members were determined to venerate and emulate
Mao. During these years, most of China was inaccess-
ible to outsiders, apart from a select few political

friends, and analysing these documents was the only way into the thinking of China's leadership.

With Mao's death in September 1976, the attraction of Mao Zedong Thought began to fade. The Communist Party tried at first to cling to the basic idea of Marxism-Leninism, which gave legitimacy to its rule, but as China opened up, and modern capitalist enterprises were allowed to develop, the arguments and justifications of classic Marxism-Leninism seemed less and less relevant. A new slogan began to appear: 'Socialism with Chinese Characteristics'. The more China continued to modernise and the more private enterprise was encouraged, the less relevant even this slogan seemed. Nevertheless, the slogan remains in place, though it is no longer quoted as often as it was even as late as the 1990s.

Where does Xi Jinping stand on all this? In his writings, he is reticent about the Cultural Revolution, although he acknowledges that it was a time of chaos. He says little about Mao Zedong personally. However, in his speeches he regularly makes ritual obeisance to the ideological tradition that preceded him. In November 2012, he insisted that, 'We should not abandon Marxism-Leninism and Mao Zedong Thought; otherwise we would be deprived of our foundation.' The following year he said, 'We must follow the guidelines of Marxism-Leninism Mao

Zedong Thought, Deng Xiaoping Theory, the important thought of the Three Represents, and the Scientific Outlook on Development.' These last two seem particularly meaningless, but they refer to the attempts by Jiang Zemin and Hu Jintao respectively to make important theoretical contributions. They were not successful: Hu's 'scientific outlook' does not even merit an 'important' from Xi.

Does he really believe in following these guidelines and, if so, what does it mean for his leadership? We cannot really be sure. Operating within the framework of the CCP is similar to some demanding religious organisations. It is absolutely essential to perform the rituals and honour the antecedents, but that is really only a formality and does not give any indication of Xi's thinking. It is much more revealing to look at what he has done.

The Maoist version of Marxism was authoritarian principally because the model it followed was the one pursued by Stalin in the Soviet Union. After Stalin's death in 1953 and Khrushchev's closed session speech in 1956 condemning Stalin's excesses, mention of Stalin in China became rarer, but Mao Zedong assumed that he had inherited the Soviet leader's mantle as head of the communist world. Stalin's successors in Moscow did not see things in quite the same way and their differences led to conflict between China and the Soviet Union. This Sino–Soviet dispute was ideological as the Russians did not like Mao's Marxism and there was a personality clash between Mao and Khrushchev, as well as a struggle for supremacy that culminated in a border war in 1969.

In spite of their differences, the style and organisation of the Chinese Communist Party owed, and still owes, a great deal to its Russian predecessor and mentor. As in the Soviet Union, the Chinese leadership is often characterised as either hard line or moderate. The writer Yang Jisheng – best known for his account of the Great Leap Forward fiasco in his book *Tombstone*, and a later history of the Cultural Revolution in *The World Turned Upside Down* – has tabulated what he described as the flip-flopping between the two extremes in PRC politics. He has demonstrated how a period of hard-line rule was often followed immediately by a period of softer or more moderate rule before it flipped back the other way. Does this mean that once Xi Jinping has finished his term of office, whenever that happens, that China will move swiftly back to a more open-minded approach? Only time will tell and many in China live in hope, even though political prudence obliges them to hold their tongues.

Some have refused to be silenced and the fate of
Xu Zhangrun, a law lecturer at the prestigious Tsinghua University in Beijing, is a case in point. In 2018,
Xu was suspended from teaching after he wrote an
article criticising the decision to allow Xi Jinping an
extension to his term of office as president. In a
follow-up article in early 2020, he condemned the
failure of the CCP to control the Covid outbreak
and criticised Xi, although indirectly by referring to
him as the 'core leadership'. He was dismissed by
Tsinghua University and blocked from publishing
critical articles on the internet. Another dissident
and former lecturer at the Beijing University of Post
and Telecommunications, Xu Zhiyong, called for Xi
Jinping to step down as leader, arguing that he was
politically inept and not very bright. At a trial held
in private, Xu was convicted of subversion and sentenced to imprisonment for 14 years.

Authoritarian political rule is often contrasted
with the democratic alternative. It is very important
to remind ourselves again in this context that China
has absolutely no tradition of democracy or a democratically elected parliament. There have been plenty
of Chinese thinkers and activists arguing for democracy, but so far they have been unsuccessful in having
it accepted as the right and proper way by which

China should be governed, with the exception of Taiwan since 1986.

Imperial China was run by authoritarian despots for centuries. Confucianism, the political thought that developed from the ideas of ancient Chinese philosopher Confucius, has served to bolster the idea of paternalistic authoritarian rule.

When the Republic of China replaced the Chinese Empire in 1912, there were demands for democracy and some concessions were made towards the creation of an electorate. Elections were held in some provinces in the early years of the twentieth century, with a very limited electorate, but generally the rulers of Republican China had military, nationalist and authoritarian backgrounds.

That is not to say that there haven't been attempts at opening up to a more democratic way of running the Chinese Communist Party and the country. There have always been individuals, and sometimes groups, within the CCP who could be described as moderates, liberals or even democrats. But they have never been more than a minority and under Xi Jinping they have been virtually silenced. The most important examples of these moderate politicians were two party general secretaries in the 1980s: Hu Yaobang and his successor, Zhao Ziyang. Both tried to push for democracy within the CCP and both were purged from the party; a warning to any future democratically inclined dissenters. On the whole, the leaders who have supported this approach have not been successful and have had their careers cut short. And this has certainly influenced Xi Jinping.

If we look more widely at the Asian environment in which China operates, China does not really stand out as being unusually authoritarian. With Narendra Modi's Hindu nationalism in India, the Marcos and Duterte legacy in the Philippines, authoritarianism in Muslim Indonesia and the military junta in Myanmar, not to mention the authoritarian Central Asian states that emerged from the collapse of the Soviet Union, China looks like one authoritarian state in a sea of many.

Westerners frequently promote the idea of democracy for China, arguing that it would make it a better country. Because these ideas are promoted in China by foreigners, frequently by Westerners whose countries have a history of partially colonising China in the nineteenth and early twentieth centuries, these ideas have become deeply suspect in the eyes of nationalist-minded Chinese, including members of the Chinese Communist Party. These democratic ideas are often seen as a Western capitalist plot designed to weaken China – and a weak

China would once again be prey to Western capitalist and colonialist control. In March 2018, speaking at a conference of the legal 'democratic parties', which exist in China but have absolutely no power, Xi praised the one-party rule of the CCP that avoided 'power rotation and nasty competition among political parties'. He is convinced that any foreign system would not work in China and would be disastrous. Xi Jinping adamantly and openly rejects any idea that Western-style multiparty democracy can ever be introduced into China. But what sort of ideological basis is there now for ruling China? Maoism has effectively gone, although it is still ritually quoted on occasion, and Socialism with Chinese Characteristics is more or less irrelevant. These are being replaced by different forms of nationalism – although Chinese leaders would never use that term – and by authoritarian systems of rule, which seem on one level to be a modern version of Confucianism.

Xi Jinping's version of this is encapsulated in his idea of a China Dream. Vague and ill-defined, the China Dream conveniently covers a multitude of policy initiatives. On one level it is a direct counterpart, or challenge, to the American Dream, which was an attempt at summarising the national spirit of the US in the 1930s. For both, becoming a great nation was central, but the Chinese version lacks the commitment to democracy and equality of opportunity that (at least in theory) were embodied in the American Dream.

The rationale behind Xi's China Dream is to allow China to take its place on the world stage. In Xi's eyes, China should be one of the two great global powers – preferably the greatest power, succeeding what he and some political thinkers in China and elsewhere believe to be the declining influence of the US. Not surprisingly, Americans do not see it that way, whether they are conservative or liberal. The US has been the dominant world power since the collapse of the USSR and China is a serious challenger to its supremacy.

To achieve parity if not superiority, the China Dream requires the rejuvenation of the Chinese nation. This is nothing new in Chinese history. In the nineteenth century reformers began searching for ways of revitalising a weak and backward nation. The backwardness was blamed on the Manchu emperors of the Qing dynasty and the nationalist Guomindang and Communist parties were rivals with their distinct programmes for modernisation.

Having been sceptical about the lip service paid by Xi – and many others – to conventional Marxist ideology, how should we assess his China Dream?

There is no doubt that it is the trademark of his administration: there are posters everywhere, often in pastel colours that are a reminder of the propaganda of the more liberal early 1960s rather than the heavy socialist realism of the Cultural Revolution that emphasised primary colours, especially red.

The China Dream is 'the rejuvenation of the Chinese nation', Xi explained in March 2017 in a speech at the National People's Congress, reprinted in *The Governance of China.* Later in the same speech he added, 'We must take our own path, which is the building of socialism with Chinese characteristics, but it is not an easy path. We are able to embark on this path thanks to the great endeavours of reform and opening up made in the past 30 years.' He was trying to show that his China Dream was a continuation of past policies and not a sudden break. He spoke of fostering 'the Chinese spirit . . . the national spirit with patriotism at its core, and . . . the spirit of the times with reform and opening at its core'. Summing up how he wanted his Chinese Dream to be understood, he insisted that it was 'in the final analysis, the dream of the people'.

There is little in these remarks to differentiate him from Deng Xiaoping or his successors, yet his administration has been much harsher. This reflects his personality and his perception of what is needed to control China through the Communist Party, rather than anything ideological. The constant and banal repetition of the China Dream mantra appears increasingly meaningless, especially in light of the mass surveillance and draconian lockdowns of recent years. Xi Jinping's other signature policy, the Belt and Road initiative, is more tangible, and we will look at that in chapter 11.

At times, the impetus behind Xi Jinping's China Dream appears to be a direct rejection of the ideas of his predecessor, Hu Jintao, that China should become a moderately well-off and harmonious society. Xi does not object to prosperity as such but insists on unity, homogeneity and party control. However, he also quotes these terms and, ironically and whether he likes it or not, the 'harmony' (和谐 *hexie*) from Hu Jintao's slogan can still be seen every day by millions of travelling Chinese: it is the name of one of the brands of high-speed trains that run throughout China. Hu Jintao had initially been a supporter of Xi Jinping and to some extent a mentor, because of Hu Jintao's respect for Xi Jinping's father, but as time went by, Hu became the symbol of all that Xi loathed. There is little direct evidence of this as inner party omerta covers up such personal feelings, but after the brutal way in which Hu was ejected from the CCP Congress in 2022, it is difficult to come to any other conclusion. It is not entirely clear what triggered the reversal, but the moderate and collegiate style of leadership which Hu Jintao shared with his premier, Wen Jiabao, is likely to have been an important factor. Xi also deplored the degree of openness of the political discourse and the authority and influence given to private businesses under Hu Jintao, which Xi regarded as undermining the authority of the party. He has done his level best to dismantle this consensus style of leadership and to replace it with a top-down authoritarian dictatorial approach. Xi's personal aversion to the working style of his predecessor has prevailed over ideological considerations.

One major feature of Xi's authoritarianism is the application of new tools and new possibilities for mass surveillance and control in the tech age that we find ourselves in. The Cybersecurity Law of 2016 provided the legal framework for a nationwide system of internet and camera surveillance that had already been in place for some years. The effectiveness of the system was driven home to me while I was in Xinjiang in 2010. There had been serious disturbances in the regional capital Urumqi in July 2009 but not in Kashgar which was potentially more of a flashpoint. When I asked why, people pointed upwards: there was an array of cameras, fixed on the newish high buildings to the south of what was then the main square. Any attempt to demonstrate or even congregate in this open space in front of the main mosque would be spotted and stopped immediately.

Since then, the net has widened and the Covid pandemic was an ideal justification for its extension and accustoming people to register with the apps on their mobile phones for a variety of purposes. The Skynet (天网 *Tianwang*) system operates across a dozen or so provinces and officially its facial recognition capability is designed to trap criminals or fugitives. Sceptics assume that it is intended to have much wider uses, but it is far from clear how effective even an authoritarian Chinese state will be in collecting, analysing and utilising the vast quantity of data that is potentially available from the technology. This is the case within China but there has also been widespread alarm that the system could be used for espionage internationally. A social credit system, which was designed to control access to goods and services, alarmed critics of surveillance, but when it came into operation it was clearly less extensive than originally feared. Similar systems of surveillance are available in many other countries: they attract critics, but the concern expressed by analysts of surveillance in China often borders on paranoia. Even the otherwise coolly analytical Kai Strittmatter, in *We Have Been Harmonised: Life in China's Surveillance State* (2019), asserts that, 'Within its borders, China is working to create the perfect surveillance state, and its engineers of the soul are again trying to create the "new man" of whom Lenin, Stalin and Mao once dreamed. And this China wants to shape the rest of the world in its own image.' This is an alarming prospect but is not confined to China: in the West there are parallel concerns about the harvesting and potential use of data by software companies and other organisations in the private sector.

Xi has also cracked down heavily on large and influential companies, especially internet companies such as Alibaba Group, a multinational conglomerate created by Jack Ma (Ma Yun) that provides services for businesses and consumers, a system of electronic payments and access to online shopping. In 2020 the Chinese government opened an investigation into Alibaba as part of an ongoing campaign against alleged anticompetitive businesses, mainly wealthy and influential organisations that were seen as a threat to the CCP. Alibaba was forced to pay heavy financial penalties and Jack Ma disappeared from public view for many months. His reappearance at the company headquarters in Hangzhou in

March 2023 was taken as a signal that the heavy-handed regulation of internet companies might be coming to an end.

Above all, under Xi's style of governance, any kind of opposition has been stifled, any dissent is seen as mutiny, and even minor differences are forbidden because what Xi Jinping insists on is homogeneity. Dissent was regularly suppressed before Xi but not to the same degree and not with the same level of malice. Xi seems unable or unwilling to countenance the possibility of diversity, of different ways of being Chinese, different kinds of social organisation, different beliefs. For him, diversity equals dissent and dissent equals weakness.

Any opposition has been crushed and thousands of individuals have been sidelined or imprisoned, including members of religious organisations that do not accept control by the CCP. There is no organised opposition to Xi Jinping either outside the Communist Party or within, but that does not mean that everyone supports him. That is far from the case, but such opposition as exists is muted, informal and secretive: it is impossible to assess how widespread it is. Should any opposition become organised or effective, it would be eliminated immediately.

Chapter 5: Xi versus Corruption: Puritan or Pragmatist?

> Many worms will disintegrate wood, and a big enough crack will lead to the collapse of a wall.
> *Xi Jinping quoting from the* Book of Lord Shang, *April 2013*, The Governance of China

CHINA IS NO STRANGER to corruption in political and economic life. That is hardly surprising; no society is immune from abuses of wealth and power, although precisely how corruption is defined varies greatly from nation to nation. As countries have transitioned from government-planned economies to various degrees of privatisation, the opportunities for enrichment at the expense of others have expanded. This was illustrated spectacularly by the rise of the Russian oligarchs after the fall of the Soviet Union in 1991. It also happened, but with less drama, in China after Deng Xiaoping's reform and opening policies were introduced in the 1980s.

Deng overturned the policies of the Mao era when there had been little focus on corruption.

Chinese critics have always argued that this was simply because there was little money around and therefore nothing much to misappropriate. China in the 1950s and 1960s was unquestionably a developing country and part of what would later be called the Global South. Its economy was recovering from decades of war and civil war. Such corruption as existed was abuse of power, both at central government level and in the collectively owned agricultural and industrial concerns – communes in the countryside and factories and other organisations in some urban areas. Commune accountants were potentially able to exercise enormous power, and corrupt accountants exposed by fearless party officials often featured in the popular Chinese literature of the time. In rural China, cash was not much in evidence; transactions in the massive people's communes – agricultural communes made up of several villages and often thousands of people and families – were recorded in work points rather than conventional currency. A corrupt accountant could award or withhold these work points in return for political or personal favours. In spite of these problems, this period is often looked on as a kind of golden age. Property crimes, including theft, were rare and people went out of their way to demonstrate their honesty. Many Western visitors in the 1960s came home with tales of discarding a melon or an empty beer bottle in their hotel room and finding that it had followed them to their next destination in some far distant town, as the floor attendant had run after them with the discarded item and put it on the next train. Xi Jinping, who was born in 1953, and his generation were at primary and secondary school in the years of Mao and the communes and were brought up on this puritanical morality.

After the foundation of the PRC in 1949, a new and privileged class or caste of bureaucrats began to emerge. This was not unique to China. There were similar developments in the Soviet Union and Eastern Europe as clearly documented by the Yugoslav politician Milovan Djilas in his 1957 book, *The New Class*. The new class in China were leading Communist Party members and their appointees in government. There was frequent abuse of privilege, which people outside the charmed circle resented. This became clear in the Hundred Flowers period of 1956–7, when the government became alarmed at popular resentment of their privileges and encouraged criticism to defuse discontent. Mao in his oblique way ordered: 'Let a hundred flowers bloom and a hundred schools of thought contend.' They did, but Mao did not like the fragrance or the thoughts of the public. People, especially the better educated, were extremely critical of the privilege of the leaders and their views were rapidly suppressed, but not before hundreds of critical newspaper articles had been published.

When the reform and opening polices were rolled out in the 1980s, the most important factor was the reduction or removal of party controls over industry and commerce. Private enterprise, which had mostly been nationalised in the early 1950s, was now encouraged. The slogan 'to get rich is glorious', usually attributed to Deng Xiaoping, was widely circulated. When I arrived in a very rainy Nanjing in October 1983, one of the first things my colleague wanted to show me was the new private market. Zhou Guansan was a sociologist working on changes in contemporary Chinese society at the Academy of Social Sciences – sociology had only recently been recognised as a proper subject for study. Nanjing was noticeably poorer than Shanghai and there were many power cuts. Judging by the power cut (停电 *tingdian*) signs outside shops and petrol stations, this was not unusual. Before travelling to Nanjing, I had been in rural Jiangxi province and witnessed the grinding poverty of many of its small towns and villages that the CCP was desperately trying to reverse.

As the economy grew, there were more and more reports of financial corruption by party and government cadres. Many high-profile cases of senior party and government officials siphoning huge quantities of money from newly privatised enterprises into their own accounts were reported in the state-controlled press as a warning to others. Some of these cases were considered by the Chinese government to be so outrageous that the perpetrators were sentenced to death by the courts.

There are obvious parallels here with the corruption in the successor states of the Soviet Union when it broke up in 1991 and the old state enterprises were sold off, often at bargain basement prices. In Russia, and some of the other ex-Soviet countries; this created another new elite, the oligarchs. China learned from the Soviet experience and, as the Deng period reforms deepened during the 1990s, no comparable oligarch class emerged in China – although some cadres became extremely wealthy. In the countryside, which still constituted the vast majority of China's population in the 1980s, the dissolution of the people's communes in 1978 led to a chaotic and technically illegal market in the sale or leasing of agricultural land. Corruption was rampant as commune leaders and local government officials acquired land for industrial or residential developments in which vast sums of money could be made. Peasant farmers, who should have been allocated land for their own use, attempted to resist these crooked deals and China experienced thousands of mass protests and demonstrations by villagers against the corruption of the local elite. This level of corruption undoubtedly threatened the credibility and authority of the Chinese Communist Party.

As Xi rose through the bureaucracy, he became increasingly disturbed by the rapid commercialisation of China, particularly the newly rich elite who he believed had abandoned the social values that Communist Party members were supposed to embody. This is the puritanical side of Xi, who was also disturbed by social evils and vices, such as prostitution and drug abuse. Xi was not alone in this; in the late 1980s, older CCP leaders reacted angrily to the increased interest in Western culture – 'bourgeois liberalisation' or 'spiritual pollution' as they termed it. Xi was also shocked by the collapse of the Soviet Union in 1992, blaming Mikhail Gorbachev for failing to defend the Soviet Communist Party and the corruption that followed its fall.

In a speech to the Central Party School in 2007, Hu Jintao had spoken of the need to tackle corruption.

There were high-profile convictions for corruption during his administration, but Xi Jinping's approach took it to a different level. For Xi, it was and remains something of a crusade. His personal reputation is that of a 'sea-green incorruptible'. He may have been part of the privileged elite, but to date there have been no serious allegations that he personally, or any of his close family and friends, have been dishonest or unethical.

Quite the opposite in fact. On many occasions, Xi went out of his way to demonstrate his aversion to corruption. Fujian province, the part of the mainland that is directly opposite Taiwan, had a history of corrupt relations between officials and local businesses, especially the port city of Xiamen and coastal city of Ningde, which was building a reputation for the light industry including lithium-ion batteries. Xi Jinping ordered an investigation into the number of private houses built in Ningde by officials with public money. There are many stories about Xi resisting the blandishments of officials in the towns and cities that he moved to as he climbed the bureaucratic ladder. These 'sugar-coated bullets', superficially attractive but dangerous, were designed to ingratiate local officials with their new boss, but they would also have put him in their debt and potentially in their power.

One notable occasion was when Xi became party secretary in Shanghai. He was looking for somewhere for himself and his family to live in the city and local officials took him to a luxurious house on South Xiangyang Road in Shanghai – a detached Western-style property of a type that are common in Shanghai and date from the early twentieth century. It occupied something like 800 square metres of land and had a garden. The regulations for the housing of provincial officials were quite clear: the maximum size for a property was set at 250 square metres; even members of the Politburo in Beijing were not supposed to have houses bigger than 300 square metres. Xi, of course, sticking firmly to the rules, did not take the house they offered. Similarly, when Xi travelled to Hangzhou, which is only a short train journey from Shanghai, his subordinates organised a private train. He rejected this and said he would go in a fairly standard seven-seat vehicle with a few colleagues rather than in a luxurious train with an impressive entourage.

Some of Xi's relatives have been or currently are in business, which is the case with many Chinese officials. When Xi moved to Shanghai, which was the most senior appointment he had before he moved into Beijing and the Politburo, those members of his extended family who had businesses in the city moved elsewhere to avoid conflicts of interest. More importantly, they were demonstrating that they were avoiding such conflict of interest.

Xi Jinping was able to sustain these anticorruption policies and campaigns because of his old-fashioned frugality. He might have been modelling himself conspicuously on the lifestyle that Mao and his colleagues would have been obliged to follow in the Yenan caves in the 1940s, and this meant that he wasn't compromised by corrupt practices.

When he arrived in Beijing to take up post in central government, his key ally was He Guoqiang who had been head of the Communist Party Central Organisation Department – a powerful organisation that controlled the nomenklatura: the list of people who could and could not be promoted to key positions. He Guoqiang then became Secretary of the Central Commission for Discipline Inspection, the CCDI, which he ran from October 2007 to November 2012. The CCDI, under He and his successor, was indispensable to Xi as the enforcement arm of his campaign against corruption.

In January 2013, Xi made a long speech to the staff of the CCDI to instruct them that they had to 'combat and prevent corruption in a more scientific and effective way' and 'improve party conduct, uphold integrity and root out corruption'. He maintained that the party was fundamentally sound but that in some areas it was prone to misconduct and corruption, if powerful individuals violated party discipline or disobeyed the laws of the country.

What Xi did not change, and in fact re-emphasised, was the belief that the party supervised its own conduct. This remained the guiding principle for controlling corruption within the party: in other words, it wasn't subject to external regulation by any government body or, more importantly, by the courts, which the party ultimately controls in any case. An independent court system is regarded as essential in democratic societies. Authoritarian regimes, such as Nazi Germany and the Soviet Union under Stalin, have subjected the judiciary to political control and China has a similar model. This is a universal concern. In recent years, there have been struggles to maintain independent court systems against attempts by right-wing regimes in Hungary, Poland and, most recently, Israel to control them.

As we have seen, Xi was able to act against corruption because of his personal, frugal lifestyle. At least as important is the fact that he did not belong to any particular Communist Party faction. This gave him free rein to deal with corruption in any wing of the party, or indeed with anyone who disagreed with his policies and could be accused of corruption. There was political calculation in this and many of those purged were potential opponents. While his anticorruption campaigns were based on genuine concerns, they were critically important in strengthening Xi Jinping's control over the Communist Party.

In the January 2013 speech that launched his campaign, Xi emphasised his determination to eliminate the big game, the 'tigers', among the corrupt in the party as well as the smaller fry, the 'flies'. These words are now associated primarily with Xi. The biggest of the 'tigers' fell from grace in the very early years of Xi's reign as general secretary. Bo Xilai had been a serious rival to Xi. In the coffee shops attached to bookshops in Beijing that were popular with young academics, Bo was being touted as a candidate for premier instead of Li Keqiang. Bo had become party secretary in the municipality of Chongqing, where from 2008 he ran a strange campaign that combined a ferocious crackdown on organised crime with a revival of Cultural Revolution period 'Red Culture', including the publicising of revolutionary songs and films from the era of Mao Zedong. Although this seemed completely anachronistic, it was surprisingly popular with people in Chongqing. I was in Chongqing in the autumn of 2011 for research on the life of Deng Xiaoping. By this time, the campaign was cooling off. The local museum had a predictably nationalistic display of Chongqing's revolutionary history, but there was also great interest in luxury shopping, notably expensive and Western-style wedding dresses. The Red Culture campaign had a dark side and even the local press raised concerns about the incompetence of the Chongqing police and their brutal treatment of people wrongly suspected of links with organised crime.

In November 2011, British businessman Neil Heywood was found dead in his hotel room in Chongqing and local authorities attempted to cover up how he had died. Early the following year, the CCDI arrived in Chongqing to investigate Wang Lijun, the police chief, and the local force under his command. To general shock and disbelief, Bo Xilai's wife, Gu Kailai, who had had a business relationship with Mr Heywood, was arrested. She was subsequently convicted of his murder and was sentenced to life imprisonment. There is no doubt that she was implicated in the murder, but Xi and his supporters were quick to use the opportunity to get rid of a rival. Bo himself was charged with taking bribes and embezzlement and also imprisoned for life. As if that were not enough, the trial of Bo Xilai implicated an even more powerful 'tiger', Zhou Yongkang, a supporter of Bo Xilai, who was secretary of the powerful

Central Commission for Political and Legal Affairs. Zhou was convicted of abuse of power, bribery and deliberate leaking of state secrets: his sentences amounted to a life in prison. The message was clear: however powerful the 'tiger', Xi's CCDI would take him down – unless, of course, he was an indispensable political ally.

Xi learned quickly from this political crisis. It reinforced his belief in the need to combat corruption, but it also persuaded him that there was much underlying sympathy and nostalgia for the years of Mao Zedong and Red Culture, when life was simpler and apparently less corrupt. Building on Bo Xilai's use of the media, television crime dramas were created to reinforce Xi's campaign. For example, the plot of *The Knockout*, a 39-episode programme, revolved around the enduring rivalry between an honest policeman and a corrupt crime boss. It was extremely popular, partly because people knew that it was based on reality. Publicity photographs for the series showed peasants sitting in their homes watching *The Knockout* beneath wall posters of Mao and Xi. The combination of a powerful anticorruption campaign, the fall of a dangerous rival, and close association with the image of Mao could only benefit Xi.

Chapter 6: Targeting Poverty: The Real Xi Revealed?

> With confidence, even barren clay can
> be turned into gold.
> *Xi Jinping*, Qiushi Journal *(Central
> Committee bimonthly) July 2022*

THE POPULAR IMAGE OF China today is of a modern prosperous society with an economy that is the envy of the world. But that is not the whole story. China has been dogged by poverty for centuries and the policies of the CCP have not completely solved the problem although there has been considerable progress. Is Xi Jinping simply an autocrat craving status and power, or is there more behind his political rise? Is it possible to determine whether issues such as poverty alleviation drive his policies and his political activity? As we have seen, the idea most commonly associated with Xi Jinping is now his China Dream (中国梦 *Zhongguo meng*). But Xi Jinping's China Dream is not just a personal vision. It is a continuation of the hopes and fears of Chinese thinkers for a century and a half who would think of themselves as patriotic or nationalist. In a speech written soon after he became general secretary of the Communist Party in 2012, Xi Jinping repeated the well-worn arguments that political divisions and backwardness had left China vulnerable to attack by Japan in the 1930s, and that this could happen again. Only development could make China strong. The idea of development for national strength is fundamental to Xi's thinking but he also believes that the levels of poverty that China still experienced in the twentieth century when he was growing up were completely incompatible with a country determined to be one of the greatest world powers. This thinking is not entirely, or even primarily, humanitarian. There are hard political calculations behind it, but his experiences in the 1970s touched him personally and profoundly affected his views on what needed to be done about poverty in China.

These experiences were primarily the four years that he spent during the Cultural Revolution as a rusticated youth in northern Shaanxi province. Shaanxi is in the less developed northwest of China and, even today, the west remains far less developed than the eastern regions. Although it was in the prosperous eastern provinces of Fujian and Zhejiang that Xi built his government and party career, his speeches and his writing show that he still had, in the back of his mind, his experiences in those poorer areas of western China. When he became a senior leader in the 2000s, he acknowledged that poverty was still a problem, paying the medical expenses for an old Shaanxi acquaintance who otherwise would not have been able to afford them. After that, it was part of his working practice to make regular inspections and visits as often as possible to all parts of the areas in which he worked. He made a point of including in his schedule the most impoverished and remote communities, which existed and still exist in even the most prosperous provinces.

How poor is China really? More often than not, it is depicted as a modern urban society with high-rise apartments, glittering shopping malls and a relatively prosperous and sophisticated population. But that is not the whole truth and part of the problem is the image that China projects to the outside world. Poverty is seen as embarrassing and shameful in what should be a great and glorious civilisation. The reality is that for most of the twentieth century, China was considered a developing country, primarily agricultural, and with major problems of often abject poverty. When the reform and opening programme launched by Deng Xiaoping began to take effect in the late 1980s, and especially after it really took off in the 1990s, there was rapid economic growth and urbanisation. Many of the poorer areas were developed and living standards improved, but the economic benefits from the programme were not equally distributed and many places were left behind.

During the 1990s, as international bodies became more aware of the outward signs of China's modernisation, people began to view China differently – it was no longer seen as an economically developing country. Official statements from the Chinese government tended to emphasise the successes of China's modernisation and risked obscuring the complex reality of rural poverty and urban opulence. In 1981, a Swedish student, whose parents had recently returned from a 'friendship tour', assured me that there was now no poverty in China. The Chinese media and official spokespeople took pains to downplay the pockets of poverty that remained. By the time Xi came to power, he was claiming that extreme poverty was a thing of the past, but he well knew that it was far from being eliminated.

Chinese colleagues could not understand why, wherever I travelled in their country, I wanted to photograph old buildings and the unmodernised traditional neighbourhoods of villages and towns. Many felt that I should have been concentrating on the new, and sometimes garish, constructions of which they were proud. My insistence that as a historian I wanted a complete picture of how these communities really looked, especially if they reflected traditional styles of building, was treated with some scepticism. Surely, I was just failing to record the progress China was making?

In the 1980s wide-ranging travel became possible within China, as did studying in Chinese universities and working with Chinese colleagues, for the first time in decades in many cases. I was able to travel and carry out research into the history of China in many different parts of the country. These were always fascinating and often remote. In China's northwest I spent much time in Ningxia and Gansu, home to the Chinese-speaking Muslim Hui communities. I sat with the local CCP secretary and mayor in Ningxia's Jingyuan County as they boasted of their success in managing disputes between different Muslim groups, lunched off tough chicken legs with Sufi shaykhs in a remote hillside shrine in the Ningxia countryside and saw for myself the poverty in this area.

As I sat with colleagues outside a restaurant in Wuzhong for supper one evening in the 1980s, they deliberately over-ordered food so that there would be extra to give to the homeless and hungry children who had gathered close to our table, who would otherwise not eat that evening. The previous week in Beijing, I had been taken to one of the most luxurious hotels in the capital. The contrast could hardly have been greater. This was an extreme case, but it illustrated the disparity between the rich, urban east of China and the poor rural west.

The east and west divide is perhaps too simplistic, however. In December 2012, soon after becoming general secretary, Xi Jinping spoke about the disparity that he witnessed during an inspection tour of Fuping County in Hubei province, which is in central China. The question of poverty was still in the forefront of his mind; he spoke of the need for the elimination of poverty and accelerated development in impoverished areas like Fuping. China, he insisted, needed to improve the livelihood of the people. This sounds innocuous and uncontroversial, but the 'livelihood of the people' is precisely the term that was used by the revered nationalist leader Sun Yat-sen in his *Three People's Principles* in the 1920s to indicate one of his key political priorities. Xi, like the rest of the CCP, reveres Sun as a founding father of modern China.

In his Fuping speech, Xi Jinping reminded his audience that it was 'the essential requirement of socialism to eradicate poverty' and the party should pay particular attention to people 'in straitened circumstances'. He noted that the numbers in poverty were quite large but that was because China was still in the primary stage of socialism. Xi went on to say that, while everywhere in China needed to concentrate on building a moderately prosperous society, 'the hardest and most arduous tasks [lay] in the rural areas and the poverty-stricken regions in particular'. Fuping was one of those areas and it was the job of the local Communist Party committee to deal with this by tackling the basic problems of jobs, education and housing.

He used the term 'moderately prosperous society', which was one of the key slogans of Hu Jintao, his predecessor. In the early years of Xi Jinping's term of office as general secretary, he did not criticise his predecessors. He even paid lip service to the peculiar and difficult to comprehend Three Represents ideology of Jiang Zemin and did not forget to remind people that they had to continue honouring the enduring spirit of Mao Zedong Thought. He was presenting himself as continuing their work and stressing the idea of unity and continuity.

That would change drastically in some of his political decisions but not in regard to poverty. Xi's commitment to poverty alleviation is long standing and genuine. His book *Cast off Poverty* (摆脱贫困 *Baituo pinkun*) is a collection of essays and speeches on the same theme, first published in 1992, and then republished in 2014 after Xi had become CCP general secretary. Some of the articles were written as far back as 1988 and most relate to his work in Fujian province. They highlight the reality of pockets of desperate poverty in what was becoming one of China's wealthiest provinces. The book's illustrations show an improbably young-looking Xi Jinping leading work teams, meeting farmers' leaders in Ningde and other parts of rural Fujian. He is also shown taking part in 'voluntary' manual labour, in photographs that replicate thousands of other images taken of his illustrious predecessors including Mao Zedong and Deng Xiaoping.

China has made great strides in the alleviation of poverty, but much work remains to be done, especially in the more remote areas of western China. Although much of the work predates his rise to power and began with the reform and opening policies of Deng Xiaoping in the 1980s, Xi Jinping deserves credit for his contribution.

Chapter 7: Crushing Democracy in Hong Kong

It is a universal rule in the world that political power must be in the hands of patriots. No country or region in the world will allow unpatriotic or even traitorous or treasonous forces and figures to seize power.

Xi Jinping, handover of Hong Kong 25th anniversary speech as reported by CNN, *July 2022*

THE CCP HAS NEVER accepted the need for multi-party democracy. The democracy movement of the 1980s ended in disaster when the PLA destroyed the demonstrations in Tiananmen Square on 4 June 1989.

But Xi Jinping's treatment of Hong Kong betrays a significant shift in his political style. It is one of the clearest illustrations of his authoritarian mentality and antipathy towards diversity and variety. Although Beijing never used force directly in Hong Kong during the crisis of 2019–20, the threat of military intervention by the People's Liberation Army always loomed in the background. It was the Hong Kong police that suppressed demonstrations and occupations on the orders of Carrie Lam, Xi Jinping's chief executive officer, and on the orders of John Lee, former senior police officer and Lam's secretary of security who succeeded her in 2022. By the spring of 2020, the democracy movement had been completely crushed.

Xi Jinping remained in the background as this crisis unfolded, but there is no doubt that he was pulling the strings. His chosen puppet was Carrie Lam who has taken the blame for the suppression of Hong Kong's pro-democracy movement, even though once appointed she had little say in policies. Beijing moved key political and military leaders to Hong Kong or nearby Shenzhen and no action was taken by Carrie Lam or her administration without the agreement or under the instructions of Beijing's officials.

We must remember, though, that Hong Kong has never had a democratic political system. This uncomfortable truth is often forgotten in discussions of Beijing's suppression of the democracy movement. Hong Kong had been a British colony since 1842 and the British governor was accountable, not to the people of Hong Kong, but to the British crown. Some representative bodies were created in Hong

Kong, notably the Executive Council (Exco) and the Legislative Council (Legco), but these were not elected by the majority of the people of Hong Kong. By and large, the government of Hong Kong represented the interests of the colonial authorities and foreign businesses. Initially, local Chinese people were excluded from these bodies, but as the Chinese business community in Hong Kong became wealthier and more influential, they were able to insist on their representatives sitting on these decision-making bodies.

Throughout British rule there were opportunities for extending representation and for introducing some kind of democratic system, but these were never taken. The most ambitious were those overseen by the final governor Chris Patten. These reforms were essentially compromises that made the ruling bodies more socially and ethnically inclusive, but they did not amount to universal suffrage.

To summarise the evolution of modern Hong Kong, its colonial history ended in 1997 when it was returned to the mainland as a Special Administrative Region (SAR). That handover, which was entirely legitimate, is now sometimes referred to as the 'first handover'. The 'second handover' refers to the changes enforced by Beijing with the introduction of the National Security Law in June 2020. The 1997 handover was based on clauses in the original 1842 Treaty of Nanking (Nanjing in modern spelling) and the 1898 Second Convention of Peking (Beijing) signed between the Imperial Chinese government and the British, and then on negotiations in the 1980s between Beijing and the Conservative government of Margaret Thatcher in London. Complex negotiations resulted in a compromise that was deemed acceptable by both sides – 'one country, two systems'. Hong Kong would become part of China as a Special Administrative Region, while retaining much of its distinctive culture and administration for at least 50 years. This meant that it would be part of China but would be able to operate its own political and legal systems, schools and colleges, postal service, and many other institutions, in its own distinctive way.

This hybrid culture was anathema to many nationalist-minded CCP officials from the mainland who were increasingly encountered in Hong Kong. At a conference at Hong Kong's University of Science and Technology as far back as 1995, I heard one visiting Chinese delegate expressing his outrage that discussions were taking place in English and not Chinese.

As a Crown Colony, Hong Kong had its own currency, the Hong Kong dollar, and issued its own

postage stamps. Originally, the stamps carried images
of the head of the reigning British monarch but, as
the inevitability of the handover loomed in the 1980s,
the monarchy became less prominent and stamp
design increasingly emphasised aspects of Hong
Kong culture and society. After the handover in 1997,
this trend continued with stamps labelled China,
Hong Kong. One issue in particular irked mainland
Chinese officials. In 2008 there was a special issue of
stamps featuring the Hong Kong judiciary, some of
which portrayed judges in their traditional, and very
British, robes. This was accompanied by a special
and well-attended exhibition at the Central Post
Office near the harbour, which emphasised the independence of the British-style judiciary.

The Hong Kong judiciary was already under
pressure from Beijing, where the judicial system is
controlled completely by the Communist Party.
Expressions of independence and Britishness did
not impress nationalistically minded Chinese politicians, including Xi Jinping.

For residents and visitors alike, there was little
obvious difference between Hong Kong before 1997
and Hong Kong after 1997, at least in most aspects
of daily life. Critics of the PRC government had predicted that Hong Kong would rapidly fall under the
rule of the Chinese Communist Party and become

just another Chinese city like its neighbour Guangzhou, or its great commercial rival, Shanghai. For
many years it looked as if this was not going to
happen but many influential figures in the Chinese
Communist Party were unhappy about the compromise, particularly the idea that the one country,
two systems compromise, which provided for genuine autonomy in Hong Kong, was due to remain in
place for 50 years. They resented what they saw as
vestiges of Western colonialism, as exemplified by
the robed judges, and pressed for a more genuine
integration of Hong Kong into the political struc-
tures of the PRC. These grievances were not a high
priority during the administrations of Jiang Zemin
and Hu Jintao. There was far greater interest in
developing the Chinese economy and to a large
extent that depended on foreign firms being able to
come and work in China as well as in Hong Kong.
Alienating foreign businesses and the many residents of Hong Kong who had come from different
countries to work was not very productive.

This changed after Xi Jinping came to power in
2012. The pressure to integrate Hong Kong more
closely into the mainland, particularly its judicial
system, police and local government, had already
become more prominent in Communist Party
internal discussions, but Xi was able to drive it

through. The concept of one country, two systems was not ignored, it was simply that the interested parties emphasised different things. Beijing only thought in terms of Hong Kong being part of one country, whereas the Hong Kong administration and the British government were determined to maintain the two systems approach. Xi Jinping encouraged the former and had the support of those members of the Chinese Communist Party who resented the fact that, to them, Hong Kong looked foreign compared with the rest of China.

Under Hong Kong's Basic Law, which became effective from 1 July 1997, when the handover took place, there was very limited democracy. The chief executive, who replaced the governor, was not elected by the people of Hong Kong but chosen by an election committee and appointed by the Central People's Government. In other words, only candidates acceptable to Beijing – which after 2012 included Xi himself – were eligible to take office. Exco and Legco, the Executive Council and Legislative Council that ran Hong Kong, had limited elections under a complicated system based on what were termed geographical and functional constituencies.

Many Hong Kong people had hoped for more and demanded general universal suffrage. This divided the community of Hong Kong: people were either pro-Beijing or pro-democracy although there was a third group, sometimes known as the Localists, who tried not to take sides but instead promoted their own local interests in Hong Kong. Clauses in the Basic Law had left open the possibility of moving towards universal suffrage and, towards the end of 2014, those Hong Kongers demanding universal suffrage came together in what became known as the Umbrella movement. The distinctive yellow umbrellas of demonstrators gathering outside government offices and in other streets and squares became a familiar sight, and pro-democracy demonstrations followed in the succeeding years. These demonstrations escalated into the Occupy Central movement, Central being the major business district on Hong Kong Island as well as the site of Hong Kong's regional government offices. The Occupy Central movement went far beyond demands for universal suffrage in Hong Kong: protesters also targeted inequality and the global financial system, drawing on the experience of the 2011 Occupy movement in New York. Their campaign was designed to be one of peaceful civil disobedience, which would persuade Beijing to allow Hong Kong to move forward to genuine universal suffrage. They made one very specific demand: that the selection of the chief executive should be made more democratically. Xi, who had the last word on the selection, was unlikely to agree to this. He and the CCP leadership feared that one of their worst nightmares had come to pass – a colour revolution like those of Georgia and Ukraine but on Chinese soil.

Beijing insisted that Hong Kong's two systems must be subordinated to one country, making it clearer than ever how they intended to interpret the one country, two systems compromise. Arguments about democracy in Hong Kong featured in local district council elections and elections to Legco in 2015 and 2016. Many of the activists were prosecuted and some were imprisoned. Carrie Lam was nominated chief executive in 2017, an appointment that could only happen if she had the full approval of Beijing and Xi Jinping. She demonstrated her loyal support for Xi Jinping's policies throughout the developing crisis in Hong Kong by executing Xi's orders.

That crisis came to a head in 2019 with an extradition bill that Carrie Lam, on behalf of Xi Jinping, pushed through the Hong Kong legislature. This bill attracted intense opposition because it permitted the authorities to extradite Hong Kong people to the mainland where they could be tried in the courts of the People's Republic of China. There is no independent judiciary in China, so these courts are under the strict control of the Chinese Communist Party. The judiciary in Hong Kong remained proud of their independence from the government of Hong Kong, never mind the government of China, and strove very hard to retain this independence. Ironically, the case that impelled the bill had nothing to do with Hong Kong and the mainland but Hong Kong and Taiwan. A Hong Kong resident had been accused of killing his pregnant girlfriend in Taiwan and could not be extradited under existing legislation.

Demonstrations against the bill increased; there was some violence and the demonstrations continued until the spring of 2020. The divisions in Hong Kong between those supporting the democracy movement and those supporting the Beijing government became sharper. In the tradition of the colour revolutions of the early twenty-first century, the people of Hong Kong and businesses were colour coded. The yellow were pro-democracy and took their colour from the yellow umbrellas of the original Umbrella movement; the blue were pro-CCP, and the blue probably came from the colour of the Hong Kong police uniforms: the physical clashes on the streets of Hong Kong were between the Hong Kong demonstrators and the Hong Kong police. The scale of the demonstrations, the occupation of some university campuses and in particular the storming of the Legco building by demonstrators alarmed Xi Jinping and the government in Beijing and their response on the street was tougher policing, the use of water cannon and many arrests.

Their political response was the introduction of the National Security Law in June 2020. This new legislation gave the Hong Kong government, the Chinese government and the police much greater powers to suppress what were becoming increasingly violent demonstrations. The effect was to put Hong Kong more firmly under the control of Beijing – a 'second handover' in the eyes of some Hong Kongers.

But where was Xi Jinping while this crisis was unfolding? In all these developments, it was Carrie Lam, as the chief executive, who was the main instigator on the ground in Hong Kong and the primary target of the demonstrators. No one doubted that, during the entire crisis, she was acting on the instructions of Xi Jinping. By keeping out of the limelight, Xi could insist that the suppression of the democracy movement in Hong Kong was being carried out by Hong Kong people. There was clearly some support for this in Hong Kong, which had become a divided city with its 'yellow' and 'blue' businesses.

Demonstrators accused Carrie Lam of lying to the people of Hong Kong and being a mere puppet for Xi Jinping. Speaking to a select group of business-people at a closed meeting as early as September 2019, she conceded that she had 'very limited' room to resolve the unfolding crisis. She went on to apologise for her role in creating the crisis – by insisting on the extradition bill – and indicated that if she had a choice she would resign, but she did not have that choice.

Xi Jinping finally emerged to speak on Hong Kong in 2022 as Carrie Lam approached retirement. He travelled to Hong Kong to attend events celebrating 25 years since the handover and congratulated the chief executive on her work.

> "With the firm support of the central authorities, Lam has faithfully fulfilled her constitutional responsibilities as the chief executive and unswervingly implemented the 'one country, two systems' policy and the Basic Law of the HKSAR over the past five years. Lam has led the HKSAR government in exercising law-based governance and united people from all walks of life to end violence and chaos and restore order in Hong Kong, fight COVID-19 and integrate into national development."

This was evidence enough that Carrie Lam was doing Xi's bidding. Xi expressed his hope that she would actively support the incoming chief executive and the new-term HKSAR government in exercising law-based governance and continue to contribute to the development of Hong Kong and the motherland. Her successor as chief executive is John Lee Ka-chiu, Secretary for Security in Carrie Lam's administration during the suppression of the disturbances, and previously Deputy Commissioner in the Hong Kong Police Force. For many pro-democracy Hong Kongers, the city had really become a police state. Xi had realised his aim of 'homogenising' Hong Kong, or at least forcing it to behave more like most cities on the Chinese mainland. In astute and subtle manoeuvres he had also ensured that it would be local leaders, and not Xi himself, who would appear responsible.

Chapter 8: Threatening Taiwan: Reality or Bluff?

> The Taiwan question is the core of the core
> interests of China . . . Those who play with fire on
> Taiwan will eventually get themselves burned.
> *Qin Gang, speech given at the Lanting Forum as
> reported by the* Financial Times *and PRC
> Ministry of Foreign Affairs, April 2023*

TOWARDS THE END OF April 2023, Taiwan was more or less encircled by a dozen mainland Chinese naval vessels including the aircraft carrier, *Shandong* (山东). The island's airspace was overflown by almost a hundred military jets. This was in response to a visit by the president of Taiwan, Tsai Ing-wen, to the US where she was due to meet the speaker of the House of Representatives, Kevin McCarthy. Commentators unfamiliar with the history of similar intimidations of Taiwan by the PLA immediately raised fears of an invasion and accused Xi Jinping of expansionist ambitions. These concerns are not new; Western fears about Chinese expansion go back decades. But how dangerous were those new exercises really and why is Taiwan so important to Beijing?

Xi Jinping's work in Fujian province while he was rising through government and party positions gave him an exceptional opportunity to understand China's complex relationship with Taiwan affairs. It is the province directly across the straits from the island of Taiwan. The chance to deal directly with Taiwanese business and political leaders was on a scale that would not have been possible in other provinces. Given this experience, the aggressive rhetoric that has emerged from CCP circles during his administration on combatting the 'independence' of Taiwan has been both surprising and alarming.

During the rollercoaster economic growth of the 1990s business and labour contacts with Taiwan expanded considerably and many Taiwanese were working in the province. Xi's provincial administration encouraged development from Taiwan and cultivated good relations with Taiwanese business-people. This was particularly apparent in the great port city of Xiamen (previously known as Amoy), where the first Taiwanese chamber of commerce in China was inaugurated while Xi was working in Fujian.

As he was rising through the ranks in the coastal provinces during the 1990s, Xi Jinping had been willing to meet political leaders and other senior representatives from Taiwan, but only as long as they acknowledged the 'one China principle' and were not supporters of independence for the island. As he moved closer to the centre and the top, he had to be more cautious. Xi met the nationalist Guomindang president of Taiwan, Ma Ying-jeou, in November 2015, but it was in Singapore's Shangri-La hotel, which counted as neutral ground. They shared diplomatic courtesies and a meal, reportedly agreeing to split the bill at the end. Xi told Ma that, 'Nothing can separate us . . . We are one family . . . We are brothers who are still connected by our flesh even if our bones are broken' (as reported by the *Guardian* in November 2015). This was a momentous occasion as it was the first meeting of leaders of the Communist Party and the Guomindang since Mao Zedong met Chiang Kai-shek in Chongqing in August 1945. Xi insisted (also reported by the *Guardian* in 2015) that, 'Today will be remembered in history. Even though this is the first meeting, we feel like old friends. Behind us is history stretching for 60 years. Now before our eyes there are fruits of conciliation instead of confrontation.'

The game changed completely when Tsai Ing-wen, the leader of the Democratic Progressive Party (DPP), became president of Taiwan in 2016; it was no longer possible to have such a meeting. Tsai is a passionate advocate of genuine independence for the island, and indeed this is a central plank of the DPP's political platform, in contrast to the Guomindang's ideology of Chinese unification. She stands out as the only woman who has reached such a senior position in Taiwan political life and has attracted unfavourable comment for her single status, her support for gay rights and, even more bizarrely, for keeping cats, with which she has been often photographed. In 2016, Wang Weixing, a senior official at the PRC Ministry of Defence, argued that Tsai lacked the 'emotional balance provided by romantic and family life' (as the *Washington Post* reported in May 2016). The Taiwan foreign minister Joseph Wu sprang to her defence, arguing that 'cat diplomacy' was an effective counter to the wolf warriors of the mainland. She is a lawyer and a legal scholar, and her speeches are calm and rational, in contrast with some of the wilder rants of China's more excitable diplomats.

For Xi, it is not possible to negotiate with the DPP, because it does not accept the principle that there is only one China. The stated position of the DPP is that Taiwan and outlying islands constitute an independent Republic of China based on Taiwan and that this should be recognised by the international community. Such an acknowledgement is anathema to the

CCP as it would acknowledge that there is a second China. Although Taiwan's de facto independence is undeniable, it is still denied the formal recognition as an independent state. A further complication is the commitment of the United States to defend Taiwan under its Taiwan Relations Act of 1979. The US backed the Guomindang regime in Taiwan against the CCP from 1949 and US finance was absolutely critical in Taiwan's rapid economic development. The American determination to defend its client democracy is unsurprisingly treated with great suspicion in Beijing, where it is seen as a cynical attempt to split China.

It is absolutely fundamental to Xi Jinping's idea of a China Dream that a rejuvenated China must take its rightful place in the world as one of the greatest nations, if not the greatest, on Earth. An essential element of this is that China must be able to control all the territory that rightfully belongs to China. While the extent and boundaries of some of that territory may be disputed by foreigners and even some Chinese scholars, Xi Jinping and the leadership of the Chinese Communist Party have no doubts at all. Their view is that all the land controlled by the Chinese Empire between the eighteenth century, when it reached its maximum size, and 1911, when it fell, belongs by right to China today. That territory includes Tibet and Xinjiang, which are currently ruled by the People's

Republic of China. Some would still include Mongolia, which the Qing dynasty and recent Chinese national-ists claim as legitimate territory. Since Outer Mongolia became independent in 1911 and was a communist state from 1924 to 1991, the PRC no longer claims that territory. Inner Mongolia is still part of China and is home to far more Mongols than its northern neighbour, but relations are on the whole peaceful.

The Chinese Empire of the Qing dynasty also included Taiwan, at least for a few years, and the CCP claims the island as an irredentist region, which must eventually return to the motherland. This is not just Xi Jinping's personal view, although it is difficult to say whether he is genuinely the epitome of the more nationalistic elements within the Chinese Communist Party – the super patriots – or if he is adopting that position for reasons of political expediency. His main preoccupations, as we have seen, are not international but domestic. However, the question of Taiwan arouses great passions in China and it is usually treated as a domestic issue although, seen from the outside, it is clearly also an international matter.

By the time Xi Jinping came to power in 2012, Hong Kong and Macau, which were never controlled by the Communist Party as they were colonies of Britain and Portugal, had returned to the mainland in handovers in 1997 and 1999 respectively.

Taiwan is not, and has never been, under the control of the Chinese Communist Party. It is a thorn in the flesh to Xi Jinping and a source of enormous irritation to the party and its government. The CCP argues that it is an inalienable part of China as it has always been Chinese. That argument does not stand up to close scrutiny.

Until the seventeenth or even the eighteenth century, there were few Chinese people on the island of Taiwan. The original population was linguistically and culturally related to their Southeast Asian neighbours in the Malayan and Filipino archipelagos. From the eighteenth century onwards, a steady flow of Chinese speakers migrated from the coastal province of Fujian to settle on the island. These Chinese colonisers spoke Fujianese, also known as Hokkien. More precisely they spoke the dialect of the south of Fujian province, Minnan. This Taiwanese Hokkien is today the native language of about 70 per cent of the population, the rest being Mandarin speakers.

The original inhabitants are today a minority on the island. They live predominantly in the south and centrally where some make a living from the tourist trade around scenic areas like Sun Moon Lake. Since the DPP came to power, their existence and rights have been openly acknowledged. Streets in Taipei have been named after them and there is a museum devoted to Taiwan aboriginal culture.

Taiwan eventually became a prefecture of Fujian province in 1683. This happened because the most powerful political figure in Taiwan, the legendary Zheng Chenggong, also known as Koxinga, who was more a bandit chief than an official, had died in 1662 and his heir and successor had died in 1681. What had been described by Chinese officials as a bandit stronghold finally became vulnerable to Chinese control. Even then, it did not become a full province of China until 1887. In 1895 the Sino–Japanese War came to an end. Japan was victorious and, as part of the spoils of war, it acquired Taiwan and ruled it as a colony until 1945. Taiwan was therefore a full Chinese province for only eight years and a colony of Japan for some fifty years.

Taiwan people are not enthusiastic about joining the mainland. Not surprisingly, the influence of Japan on the culture of Taiwan is very strong and it remains apparent today. Taiwan in this colonial period looked two ways. There were family, cultural and business ties with Fujian on the mainland and some of those ties remain, but Japan was the model of modernisation for many Taiwanese. It was to Japan that they looked for advanced technology, for political ideas and for modern lifestyles. In many ways, this is still the case.

Television soap operas from Japan and especially from Japan's other former colony Korea are more popular in Taiwan than anything from mainland China.

The closeness of Taiwan with Japan is also indicated by the number of Taiwanese people who served with the Japanese army in the years that Japan was expanding and colonising large parts of Asia, including China. Taiwanese recruits to the Japanese army included Lee Teng-hui, later president of Taiwan, who was also educated at a Japanese university, and his elder brother who was killed in Manila while serving with the Imperial Japanese Navy. These connections are anathema to the Chinese Communist Party, which bases its right to rule China partly on their resistance to the Japanese invasion of mainland China in the 1930s.

When Japan was defeated at the end of the Second World War in 1945, the Asian world changed dramatically. Under the 1943 Cairo Declaration and the 1945 Potsdam Proclamation, Taiwan was to be returned to China, together with all other Chinese territories occupied by the Imperial Japanese Army. Since Taiwan had only been a province of China for eight years, the use of the word 'returned' was questionable, but China under Chiang Kai-shek was an ally of the US, Britain and the USSR and had to be compensated.

'Returning' Taiwan was complicated by the civil war in China between the Chinese Communist Party and the nationalist Guomindang. By 1948, the Guomindang were clearly losing and had moved their administrative and military headquarters from the mainland to Taiwan. The existing Chinese population of Taiwan who spoke Hokkien were not pleased at the invasion of a Mandarin-speaking elite that took control of the island.

At the end of the Chinese Civil War in 1949, the PRC was in control of most of the mainland and, as far as they were concerned, the Guomindang regime in Taiwan under Chiang Kai-shek, the king over the water, was an enemy base for opposition to the Chinese Communist Party. This shows the gap between the reality of Taiwan during the years Xi Jinping was growing up and the CCP contention that the island was always part of China.

Relations between the Chinese Communist Party and the nationalist Guomindang were always poor since the civil war, but they are far easier than Beijing's relations with the current government of Taiwan, the Democratic Progressive Party. The CCP would prefer Taiwan to be governed by its former political enemies, the Guomindang, simply because both of those parties accept the idea of 'one China'. The Democratic Progressive Party wishes to transform their de facto independence into de jure recognition as an independent state. They have been elected in what has been a democratic multiparty system since 1986 and they are currently the government of Taiwan. Cross-straits relations, which is the official term for contacts between Beijing and Taipei, continue but are problematic.

Relations worsened, once Xi Jinping came to power, and now he will always be associated with an increase in tensions, militarist rhetoric and political posturing. This reached its height before the Communist Party Congress of October 2022 and then again in the build-up to the National People's Congress of March 2023. Xi was determined to secure his extended term of office in the course of these two meetings and believed that his success would be assisted by aggressive posturing against Taiwan. This would certainly be supported by sections of the military, as well as the more nationalist elements of the CCP.

If Xi's rhetoric is to be taken at face value, when he came to power he was determined that, under his rule, Taiwan would be 'reunited' with mainland China. This would be a feather in his cap, something that even the great Mao had failed to do. The People's Liberation Army has deployed naval or air force units very close to Taiwan. There have also

been political provocations and some military provocations by the United States. In the West, there
have been concerns that China will copy Vladimir
Putin's invasion of Ukraine and take Taiwan by
force while the US and its allies are preoccupied.
However, this is unlikely and is usually argued by
people with little or no understanding of the unusual
situation of Taiwan. Although there are some undeniable parallels, the positions of Ukraine and Taiwan
are significantly different, principally because of the
geopolitics and the countries likely to be involved.
Taiwan has never been ruled by the CCP, whereas
Ukraine was an integral part of the USSR from
1922 until 1991. NATO did not come to the aid of
Ukraine when Russia invaded in 2022 as Ukraine
was not a member, whereas any invasion of Taiwan
would trigger retaliation by the US, supported by
Japan, South Korea and other Asian and Pacific
nations. The ensuing conflict would disrupt supplies
of silicon chips, semiconductors and other advanced
technologies, which advanced economies depend on.

There was genuine international consternation
in early April 2023 when the PLA mounted their massive operation simulating the encirclement of Taiwan
prior to an attack. This was a repeat performance of
the military exercises that followed the visit of Nancy
Pelosi to Taiwan in August 2022. The latest

manoeuvres, though substantial, were less dramatic than for Speaker Pelosi's visit, but that ships and aircraft crossed the semi-official halfway line between the island and the mainland is a reminder of the danger posed in the case of an accident. Beijing's rationale is that such visits imply formal recognition of Taiwan's government and are therefore recognition of the island's independence. As the three days of Beijing's military exercise came to an end, similar manoeuvres by American and Philippines armed forces were underway in the Pacific. Tit-for-tat provocations only served to increase tensions and the danger of a miscalculation or accident leading to armed conflict.

Replying to PRC Foreign Minister Qin Gang's incendiary statement about what would happen to anyone 'playing with fire on Taiwan', his opposite number in Taiwan, Joseph Wu (Wu Chao-hsieh), agreed that he was taking Chinese threats very seriously. He cited analysis from unnamed sources in US intelligence organisations that China was preparing a military annexation in 2027. Xi Jinping will still be in power at that time, but this is not a date that any Chinese sources have mentioned. The origins of this prediction are not clear, but they are either the result of wargaming or pure guesswork.

There are many potential flashpoints in the Asia-Pacific region that could lead to military conflict between China and the US. They include the Koreas and the islands of the South China Sea, but Taiwan is the most hazardous: an attempt by Beijing to incorporate Taiwan into the PRC by force, or a declaration of sovereignty and independence by the DPP in Taiwan, would inevitably trigger such a conflict. We should remember that the Pacific War of 1941 to 1945 was immensely costly in lives and resources: avoiding a new Pacific War is imperative.

If, however, the opposition Guomindang were to be re-elected to the presidency and control of the parliament in Taiwan, this would be an opportunity for Xi to negotiate or impose a deal to bring Taiwan into a close relationship of some sort with China. This is, of course, conjecture, but it is the type of political calculation that Xi Jinping must make.

In Taiwan itself, public opinion on any threat from China varies. Family and friends in Taiwan consistently tell me that there is not the level of panic and fear that many Western commentators and politicians suggest. They have been used to threats, alarms and air raid drills for decades. They might appear complacent but, since they have absolutely no control over the situation, carrying on with work and the serious business of making money or shopping is a rational response. Meanwhile Xi Jinping keeps everyone guessing.

Chapter 9: Uncle Xi and Winnie-the-Pooh: Cult of Personality

A political leader of the Song Jiang type.
Wu Ming, Xi Jinping zhuan *(Biography of Xi Jinping (2010)*

ONE OF XI'S BEST Chinese biographers, Wu Ming has likened the character of Xi Jinping to that of Song Jiang, whom Xi is said to admire. This is a subtle and puzzling comparison, which does not imply either compliment or condemnation. Song Jiang was a historical figure, later popularised in the Ming dynasty novel *Water Margin* (水浒传 *Shuihu zhuan*). Although the novel paints him as heroic, he is often looked down on by Chinese as two-faced: a hypocrite whose assertions of moral rectitude are inconsistent and self-serving. He was a rebel but also maintained that he was loyal to the government of the empire. According to Wu, Song Jiang was not 'a man of great talent and bold vision', but he had the ability to unite disparate groups of talented individuals. This is hardly a ringing endorsement of Xi.

Water Margin is one of the most popular of the classic Chinese novels in an accessible language. It is often compared with the Robin Hood legends of the English folk culture tradition and is based on a group of rebels sequestered in their stronghold in the marshes. Since the Chinese Communist Party's early heroic days were as rebels in the remote Chinese countryside it is hardly surprising that it is the most popular with party members.

An anonymous Beijing editor, quoted in Evan Osnos's 2015 *New Yorker* article 'Born Red', summed Xi up by saying 'He's not afraid of Heaven or Earth. And he is, as we say, round on the outside and square on the inside; he looks flexible but inside he is very hard.'

If you look at Chinese Communist Party publications, you will see everything expressed in ideological or bureaucratic terms. Opinions are presented as neutral and objective, with no suggestion that there might be valid alternatives. The part played by individuals in politics since the demise of Mao Zedong has been downplayed, largely because the personality of Mao loomed so large and so disastrously. In reality, the personalities and images of individuals do play important roles in the way the party controls the government and the nation.

The ultimate cult of personality was the adula-tion of Mao. Xi Jinping has been creating something very similar, although not on the same level of absurdity. His immediate predecessors, Hu Jintao and Jiang Zemin, had nothing approaching a 'cult of personality' – a term which emerged from the Soviet Union following the death of Stalin in 1953 and Khrushchev's denunciation of him three years later. On the contrary, following the example of Deng Xiaoping, Jiang and Hu positively avoided any simi-larities to the way Mao Zedong had ruled.

Creating images and manipulating the mass media have been crucial in getting across political messages. Once again, we need to look back to Chi-na's experience of the Mao era if we want to understand Xi Jinping in power. The important period is the Cultural Revolution, the chaotic decade between 1966 and 1976. Both Jiang Zemin and Hu Jintao have deliberately distanced themselves from this period, but Xi Jinping has at times accentuated or overstated the positive aspects of Mao's rule.

In the late 1960s and early 1970s, Mao Zedong's image was everywhere. That is not an exaggeration. His picture appeared on wall posters, placards car-ried by Red Guard demonstrators at mass rallies, in every newspaper and magazine, and on televi-sion, although TV was still in its infancy. What everybody remembers about the Cultural Revolution is the Little Red Book – *Quotations from Chairman Mao Tse-tung*. *Quotations* was treated as a sacred text. Selections had to be read aloud before meetings; all newspapers and magazines began with prominent quotes from Mao, often with little or no relevance to the contents. If you were not able to quote the more popular sayings of Mao that were included in *Quotations*, you were likely to be suspected of disloyalty to Mao. *Quotations* was drawn from the many books of Mao's writings and, in imitation of Mao, at least eight volumes of Xi Jinping's writings have appeared, including his political essays, *New Words from the Zhi River* (*Zhijiang Xin Yu* 之江新语), drawn from newspaper columns in *Zhejiang Daily*, the official newspaper of the province where the Zhijiang River flows. This is not quite *Quotations*, and he can hardly be blamed for *The Little Yellow Book: Quotations from Chairman Xi Dada* which has been published outside China.

Portraits of Mao were hung up in factories, schools, shops, and many other public and private buildings. Individual homes all had pictures of Mao on their walls; not to have one of these risked attack from Red Guard groups and accusations that you were a traitor, a class enemy and a reactionary. There was always a danger of physical violence and the risk of losing your job. In rural households especially, the portrait of Mao was placed where in traditional times there might have been a little statue of the kitchen god, the deity who was believed to watch over the house and, in some versions of folk religion, to report back to heaven on the doings of that household.

Adulation of Mao metamorphosed into Mao-worship, which had penetrated to the deepest levels of Chinese society. This was precisely what Deng Xiaoping and his successors rejected. They hoped that it had been expunged for ever. After Mao died in 1976, people gradually felt able to laugh at the juvenile excesses of the Cultural Revolution and thank their lucky stars that these were never going to be repeated.

When Xi launched his anticorruption campaign in 2013, he gradually and carefully cultivated his image as a successor, not to Deng Xiaoping, Jiang Zemin and Hu Jintao, but to Mao Zedong. The same Red Culture that Bo Xilai had used was being revived by Xi. Posters with images of Xi were often placed next to similar ones of Mao, to show that Xi was as powerful as his predecessor. Often these posters showed Xi dressing as Mao did and were prominent during Xi's anticorruption campaign. The subliminal message was that eliminating corruption could somehow recreate the simpler and more honest era of Mao's time. Since that was impossible, and a return to Maoism was not acceptable to many in the CCP, it could be implied in an image but could not be stated explicitly.

Xi has acquired various nicknames, some more respectful than others. A man with an apparently fragile ego, he detests comparisons, usually on the internet, with the Disney cartoon version of A.A. Milne's *Winnie-the-Pooh*. These comparisons arose after film circulated of Xi walking like Pooh Bear, with the hapless premier, Li Keqiang, following in his train in the manner of Pooh's sidekick, Piglet. Any such images are deleted by China's vast army of censors as soon as they appear. In April 2023, after the concentrated military activity designed to intimidate Taiwan's government, a new badge became popular in Taiwan. It was modelled on the patches worn by combat pilots and depicted a Formosan Black Bear (Formosa being an obsolete name for Taiwan) punching Winnie-the-Pooh, with the slogans 'Fight for Freedom' and the much-adored air force command for fighter pilots: 'Scramble!' Published photographs show pilots and other officers wearing the patch.

Xi has also been dubbed Xi Dada. This has been translated as Uncle Xi (presumably a nod to 'Uncle

Joe' Stalin) or Daddy Xi, although those are not standard Chinese terms. Whether this was originally Xi's idea is unclear, but the nickname has been adopted by the official media, including the powerful Xinhua news agency, to make him seem closer to the populace, but later dropped, possibly because it could imply that he was a great dictator. (Ironically in the Uyghur language of Xinjiang it means 'father', though Xi is hardly a father figure to Uyghurs.) Media outlets replaced this with Xi Yeye, Grandpa Xi, and a song, 'Grandpa Xi is our Big Friend' (习爷爷是我们的大朋友 *Xi yeye shi women de da pengyou*), was written for primary school pupils to sing.

I have looked through the several hundred photographs that I took in China in 2017 and 2018. These were all taken in Shanghai and Suzhou and, remarkably, there is not one single image of Xi Jinping in the entire collection. But since that time, Xi's image has become increasingly ubiquitous – almost as ubiquitous as Mao's. Xi is skilled at managing his image, as can be seen from the care he takes in the careful curation of his wardrobe for different occasions. Depending on his audience, he has appeared in a well-tailored version of the Sun Yat-sen suit (often called the Mao suit) or even a version of camouflaged battledress, which looks faintly absurd as he has never actively served in the military, let alone experienced combat. His image is extremely important to him.

Getting behind the official image, discerning the real Xi, is notoriously difficult. We know about his early history and we are in no doubt about his determined patriotism, his China Dream, his detestation of corruption and his attacks on poverty. But very little is known about him as a person, and almost nothing about his personal life apart from his glamorous and melodious wife, Peng Liyuan. Xi Jinping never gives interviews and those who are close to him do not speak in public. So discreet are Xi and his associates that it is not even clear who these intimates are, who he relies on, and who he trusts for advice. They may be the same people who he has chosen for the powerful Politburo Standing Committee and key posts in government, but whether his relationships with them go beyond the purely political is unclear.

He is said to respect vigorous masculinity and scorn egghead intellectuals. In formal portraits he strikes heroic attitudes and projects an image of a tough guy, although he does not go to the embarrassing extremes of Vladimir Putin, who appears shirtless and caressing weapons at the drop of a hat. At official banquets he appears to drink copious quantities of *maotai* spirit without feeling any effect, although unkind observers have suggested that this is because he primes the waiters to fill his glass with water instead.

During the Jiang Zemin and Hu Jintao administrations, it was possible to rely on the burgeoning Hong Kong publishing industry to furnish inside information, gossip – and at times pure invention – about the lives of the Chinese leadership and their activities in Zhongnanhai. When one former Hong Kong newspaper editor, 73-year-old Yao Wentian (Yu Mantin in Cantonese), prepared to publish his critical biography of Xi, he was arrested while on the mainland and imprisoned. Books and magazines about the CCP that came out of Hong Kong may have been flawed but they were at least a starting point. Now they are gone, effectively banned by regulations brought out by Xi and his administration.

The wall of secrecy that has been re-erected around the party and government compound of Zhongnanhai in central Beijing suits Xi down to the ground. His private life and deepest thoughts remain out of reach: it is really only possible to judge him on the basis of his formal speeches and articles and, more importantly, his actions.

Chapter 10: Xinjiang Behind Bars

> The Chinese authorities have created a dystopian
> hellscape on a staggering scale in the Xinjiang
> Uyghur Autonomous Region.
>
> *Agnès Callamard, Amnesty International News,*
> *June 2021*

OUTSIDE CHINA, THE TWO things that Xi Jinping
is most likely to be remembered for are the crushing
of democracy in Hong Kong and the brutal repression of the Uyghurs in Xinjiang. In both cases, these
were the culmination of long historical conflicts,
but the harsh and uncompromising manner in which
both were dealt with by Xi Jinping's administration
bore his distinctive mark. As my Chinese colleagues
never cease to remind me, Xinjiang is completely
different from the rest of China. The Uyghurs
speak a language related to Turkish, not Chinese,
and they are Muslims. They were a majority in Xinjiang, their homeland, but Chinese migration has
changed that.

Uyghurs have suffered discrimination for many decades but the mass incarceration under Xi Jinping has been so much harsher than anything they have known, and Xi and the Chinese Communist Party have been accused of genocide. Whether this is an accurate and appropriate designation is highly contentious. Beijing naturally rejects the allegation. Uyghur émigré organisations and activists who support the Uyghurs insist that Xi and the Chinese government should face charges of genocide: a book published in 2022 by Nury Turkel, a highly respected Uyghur community leader in the US and a lawyer, is entitled *No Escape: The True Story of China's Genocide of the Uyghurs.*

Major international human rights organisations have been more circumspect because of the precise meaning of the term. Both Amnesty International and Human Rights Watch usually describe China's policies as 'crimes against humanity' and some critics have used terms such as 'cultural genocide'. Although there have undoubtedly been deaths in the internment camps, there is no evidence of a deliberate policy of extermination, or that the deaths are on the scale of acknowledged genocides such as the Jewish Holocaust of the 1940s, the Rwanda massacres of the 1990s, the genocide in Namibia in 1904–8 and the Armenian genocide of 1915–17, although the existence of that genocide is denied by Turkish authorities. Many Western scholars who have worked in Xinjiang, know the languages and the people well and deeply sympathise with the Uyghurs, avoid use of the term genocide. That is also my position, and I am aware that some Han Chinese who are otherwise sympathetic to the Uyghurs have been repelled by the use of the term.

Xinjiang is a vast region in the northwest of the People's Republic of China; it is about three times as large as France. It is remote from Chinese-speaking China and, even within the region, travel is time-consuming and arduous. In the Mao period it was difficult for foreigners to travel in Xinjiang, but it opened to tourists, businesspeople and academic visitors in the 1990s.

Conflict in Xinjiang goes back hundreds of years. Until the eighteenth century, the height of the Manchu Qing dynasty, it was a peripheral society, not Han Chinese, and often in conflict with the major power of East Asia, Imperial China. From China's point of view, it was a collection of frontier city states around a forbidding desert, the Taklamakan. But this was not how the Muslim Uyghurs of Xinjiang thought of themselves. They belonged to Central Asian Turkestan, sharing culture and religion with the Kazakhs, the Kyrgyz and especially the Uzbeks, whose Turkic language is close to Uyghur.

Xinjiang did not become a province of China until 1884; even then there was considerable disagreement among the elite of the Qing dynasty as to whether it was a good idea to bring it into the imperial fold. This province was named Xinjiang at that time, meaning 'New Frontier', but for many of its inhabitants it is Eastern Turkestan. From that time onward, there have been attempts by Uyghurs and other non-Chinese communities to create, or recreate, governments in Xinjiang that are fully independent of the Chinese state. During the early twentieth century there were two serious attempts, one in the 1930s and one in the 1940s. These regimes did not last for long and the final one was subsumed within the PRC in 1949. The memory of these short-lived independent republics still lives on in the Uyghur community in Xinjiang, and in the Uyghur diaspora throughout Asia and the rest of the world. From observations and conversations in Xinjiang over the years, and the active resistance that continued until recently, it is clear to me that the desire for independence from China remains strong in the Uyghurs. This is closely connected with the desire of the Uyghurs to practise Islam openly and without restrictions. Émigrés have brought news of resistance from inside Xinjiang and this is available on websites, most of it in the Uyghur language. Any discussions of independence for Xinjiang, or criticism of Chinese rule, are dangerous for Chinese citizens and can lead to long periods of imprisonment.

Xinjiang was incorporated into the new People's Republic in 1949; this is called its 'peaceful liberation' in official accounts. In 1955, it was declared an autonomous region. The name is misleading; the autonomous status acknowledged that most of the population were not Han Chinese. There was provision in the government of the region for senior Uyghur officials but, in reality, there was little genuine autonomy. The central government in Beijing was in overall control through its Communist Party organs, which were all run by Han Chinese.

Active resistance to Chinese rule has persisted, although it has been sporadic and patchy since it was suppressed by the People's Liberation Army in the 1950s. This resistance revived during the 1960s when China fell into chaos during the Cultural Revolution and an East Turkestan People's Party was formed with a certain amount of assistance from the Soviet Union, which at that time was beginning to come into conflict with China. Even greater resistance emerged after the collapse of the Soviet Union in 1991. Former constituent republics of the USSR, such as Kazakhstan, Kyrgyzstan and Uzbekistan, became independent states in their own right.

In that case, argued many Uyghurs, why could the same not happen to Xinjiang? If there could be western Turkestan republics, why could there not be an Eastern Turkestan Republic for the Uyghurs?

Pressure for independence escalated. By the 1990s there had been many anti-Chinese demonstrations and underground organisations were formed. Many of these claimed to be armed and some had impressive or fanciful titles such as the Eagles of the Tengri Tagh, United Revolutionary Front of Eastern Turkestan, the Free Turkestan Movement and the Wolves of Lop Nor. An official Chinese list of 'separatist organisations' included the East Turkistan Islamic Movement (ETIM), the East Turkistan Liberation Organization (ETLO) and the Islamic Reformist Party 'Shock Brigade', among others. Some of these groups issued manifestos via the internet and claimed responsibility for attacks on targets associated with the Chinese state, but it is difficult to estimate how large or effective they were. The situation is confusing and in most cases it is impossible to know whether they were real organisations on the ground in Xinjiang, or just had an internet presence for propaganda purposes.

Repression by the Chinese state increased in response. There were many violent confrontations between the forces of the state and the Uyghurs throughout the 1990s but the most serious were in Ghulja (Yining in Chinese) in 1995 and 1997. These clashes triggered a new Strike Hard policy of repression from the Chinese government. This resulted in mass arrests and detentions and severe restrictions on Islamic religious activities.

I was able to visit Xinjiang on many occasions between 1990 and 2010 and worked and travelled with both Chinese and Uyghur colleagues over most of the region. I visited and spoke to many Uyghurs in Urumqi, Kashgar, Turpan and other parts of Xinjiang, sometimes with Chinese colleagues but increasingly on my own. I wrote articles on my concerns about the situation in Xinjiang for Chatham House's *The World Today* and commented on the BBC, but apart from reports by Amnesty International, Minority Rights Group and Human Rights Watch there was little interest in the repression that was becoming apparent, although Chinese diplomats did take me to lunch to explain how I misunderstood the situation. That would change dramatically after Xi Jinping's intervention in 2017.

There were no obvious signs of conflict in Urumqi on any of my visits, and I met Han Chinese who had close Uyghur friends. But Han Chinese were not popular with the locals. Regarded as interlopers, they experienced some discrimination in the shops and Chinese were often charged more than Uyghurs.

The Uyghur language was not valued by the Chinese administration. Teachers complained about the lack of textbooks and dictionaries for teaching Uyghur but material for encouraging Han officials to tackle the local languages was beginning to appear. This included a television series called *One Sentence a Week* (每周一句话 *Mei zhou yi ju hua*) with an accompanying course book and a two-volume textbook *Uyghur for the Masses* (大众维语 *Dazhong wei yu*). My friends did find a Uyghur-Chinese dictionary for me and it remains in use to this day. Uyghurs expressed their distinctive identity through their language, a strong preference for fabrics, carpets and other goods imported from Muslim countries like Pakistan and former Soviet Central Asia, and by the ubiquitous, loud and driving Uyghur popular music.

A violent confrontation between the Uyghur and the Han Chinese population of Urumqi shook the autonomous regional capital and seat of government in July 2009. Much of Urumqi looks like any other major Chinese city, but there are distinctly Uyghur areas, although these are being Sinicised. The disturbances cost perhaps hundreds of lives and the Han Chinese, who were in a minority in Urumqi but dominated the administration, put pressure on the central government to do something about the 'Uyghur problem'. It was this violence in usually peaceful Urumqi that persuaded many in the central government that a new approach was needed. It fell to Xi Jinping, who became CCP general secretary in 2012 and president in 2013, to decide on the nature of that approach.

The turning point came in 2016 when Xi Jinping transferred Chen Quanguo to Xinjiang with orders to solve the problem of Uyghur resistance once and for all. Chen had been the party secretary of Tibet for five years and had the reputation of successfully crushing resistance to the Chinese administration and reducing the number of self-immolations by Tibetan Buddhist monks and nuns.

The War on Terror that had been declared by US President George W. Bush after the September 11 attacks on Washington and New York by Al Qaeda provided governments with a new vocabulary. Any dissent or opposition could now be classified as 'terrorism'. In speeches not reported officially, Xi Jinping urged his officials to emulate Bush's 'war on terrorism', when it came to Uyghur resistance.

There were genuine reasons for forceful resistance by Uyghurs. Much of the conflict occurred when families attempted to rescue Uyghurs, particularly young men, from arbitrary arrest and imprisonment by the police. There were also attacks on police stations and government offices in retaliation.

Chen Quanguo, who reported directly to Xi Jinping, constructed a series of what was called 'convenience police posts' throughout Xinjiang. These were manned day and night and supplied with first aid kits and other equipment, ostensibly to assist in 'emergencies'. No one was fooled. The police posts had surveillance cameras and could easily be converted to checkpoints and used to block off roads and close down areas of the region in the case of conflict.

Chen introduced systems of monitoring households by requiring neighbours to spy on each other and report any unauthorised activity to the police. He also cracked down on religious activities in Xinjiang in an attempt to undermine the authority of Islam over the Uyghur population. Restaurants that would normally have closed during the daylight hours of Ramadan were forced to remain open and students who attempted to fast were bullied into eating or reported to the authorities if they persisted. There were even attempts to persuade parents not to give their children Islamic-sounding names. Similar activities, including attempts to outlaw the hijab or other outward signs of Islamic allegiance, had already been introduced piecemeal throughout, but Chen's clampdown on Xi Jinping's orders was more comprehensive than anything seen previously.

Chen Quanguo effectively closed off Xinjiang. Local people had their passports confiscated so that they were unable to travel abroad. This reflects the belief of the authorities that discontent in Xinjiang was not home grown but was deliberately fostered by outside agents. Movement around Xinjiang itself was also restricted. Religious materials, including copies of the Qur'an produced outside China, were confiscated during the spring of 2017 as part of a campaign against the ownership of illegal religious items. Oddly enough, editions of the Qur'an published in China were considered safe.

Internet access to and from Xinjiang had been controlled even more closely than in other parts of China. In the spring of 2010, it was switched off completely during my stay in Urumqi but was back on by the time I reached Kashgar. Even then, of course, it was subject to normal Chinese internet restrictions. Access was slow and many external websites were blocked but it was possible to send emails. Until the arrival of Chen Quanguo, Xinjiang had enjoyed a period of relative freedom. In 2010, mosques were open and the sound of the muezzin calling the faithful to prayer could be heard regularly on the walk from my hotel into the centre of

Kashgar. In the same year, I was able to travel to the desert shrine of Imam Asim, north of the city of Khotan, which is a 12-hour drive from Kashgar, to attend the annual shrine festival. That year was very well attended and people from Kashgar had been desperate to get to the festival, which some saw as almost equivalent to the hajj pilgrimage to Mecca. By 2016, the festival had been banned and the shrine itself levelled by the Chinese authorities on the orders of Chen Quanguo and Xi Jinping.

There were also indications of problems to come. The entire centre of Kashgar had been demolished as part of a process the authorities described as slum clearance, but Uyghurs were sure it was a way of breaking up their compact community. Kashgar was patrolled constantly by armed police.

The most serious repression began in the summer of 2017. Silently, without any public acknowledgement, Chen Quanguo ordered the creation of a network of re-education camps, which were designed to house and retrain any Uyghurs suspected of having sympathy with separatists or what the Chinese regarded as extremist religious ideas. The Chinese authorities did not announce the construction of these re-education camps; for many months, they denied that the camps even existed. Westerners were able to track their construction by satellite surveillance and online documents that revealed bids and contracts for massive new construction projects. Since the repression had begun in the 1980s or 1990s, there had always been large numbers of Uyghurs detained in prisons and labour camps in Xinjiang but not on the scale of the detentions that began in 2017. Xi Jinping, impressed by Chen Quanguo's hard-line policies in Tibet, transferred him to Xinjiang to put an end to Uyghur resistance and the camps are their chosen method.

These specialised re-education camps – which could just as easily be termed internment or concentration camps – were designed to 'deradicalise' Muslims, a term adopted by Chinese leaders, and turn them into patriotic citizens of the People's Republic of China. Evidence of the methods used, including official Chinese videos, justify calling this brainwashing, a term that originated in China in the 1950s at the time of the Korean War.

Nothing on this scale had happened before Xi Jinping came to power. It is still extremely difficult to assess the scale of these camps or the total number of people who were incarcerated. Some Uyghurs are kept in the prisons for many years. Others were held for weeks or months and sent back to their villages and towns when they were deemed to be safe to be let back into the community.

Conditions in the camps are similarly varied. There are reports of extremely harsh conditions by Uyghurs who were in the camps and have been released. The most concrete and reliable accounts have been provided by people who were able to leave Xinjiang and move to Western Europe or the United States. There are also many horror stories of torture, sexual violence and other abuses of Uyghur detainees by their guards, many of whom are likely to be Uyghurs themselves. This is a reminder that there is no simple division between Han and Uyghur in Xinjiang. There have always been Uyghurs who were willing to make a career in government organisations and that included the police and prisons. When the then president of Iran, Akbar Hashemi Rafsanjani, visited Xinjiang in September 1992, I joined the crowd waiting for him to arrive at the main Hetgar Mosque (also known as the Id Kah Mosque) in Kashgar. The crowd was controlled by dozens of police, almost all of whom were Uyghurs. There is a similar situation in Tibet. I discussed prison conditions with a Tibetan nun who had managed to leave China and she confirmed that some of the prison guards who had abused monks and nuns were Tibetans.

Some of the more disturbing accounts of brutality might be exaggerated by anti-Chinese organisations, but independent and reliable evidence of conditions across the whole network of camps is difficult to obtain. The number of individuals incarcerated has been variously estimated as being in the hundreds of thousands, possibly a million, possibly a million and a half. It is far from clear how some of these numbers have been calculated and whether they refer solely to long-term detainees or also to those who have been through the camps and returned home.

The basic problem is that China has not allowed foreign individuals or organisations access to the camps. Beijing has provided only sparse information about conditions in the camps and the policies of re-education. Some official videos that have been circulated show the humiliating and degrading treatment of Uyghurs, forcing them to sing and dance in ways that they would never do in real life: the authorities do not seem to have realised how bad an impression this gives of Chinese rule in Xinjiang.

There have been reports of many inmates becoming seriously ill and of deaths in the camps, but they are not specifically death camps. There is no decision to exterminate the Uyghurs as a people, even though the poor conditions in the camps may well be responsible for many deaths, including suicides. The policy of mass incarceration has created destruction and disorganisation in Uyghur society on a level not seen in many decades. Organisations outside China sympathetic to the plight of the Uyghurs have insisted that this mass incarceration is a form of genocide.

The detainees in the camps are drawn from all classes of Uyghur society, many from regular farming families, but the educated classes – writers, teachers, academics – have been particularly targeted.

There are two notable and egregious examples of the incarcerations of Uyghur intellectuals. One is the academic economist Ilham Tohti, who was an established and respected teacher at the Central Nationalities University in Beijing. In 2014, he was sentenced to life imprisonment and the confiscation of all his property and other assets, and accused of separatist activity, the term used for anyone advocating an independent Eastern Turkestan. He had done no such thing: his crime was to maintain a website in which he discussed with fellow Uyghurs and others possible options for resolving the conflict in Xinjiang. Simply by attempting to have a discussion independent of the narrative controlled by the Chinese Communist Party, he was deemed to be a 'terrorist' or separatist (which, under the new definition, were essentially the same thing). The other is the anthropologist Rahile Dawut, who is well known for her research on the history and sociology of

Islamic shrines in Xinjiang which she has published in both Chinese and the Uyghur language. She remains in prison and almost nothing has been heard of her for many years. Some of the shrines she has documented have been destroyed by the Chinese authorities, including the impressive Imam Asim shrine high in the Taklamakan desert north of Khotan. It was fully functioning when I joined pilgrims at the shrine festival in May 2010, but photographs indicate that it has since been bulldozed in an episode of cultural vandalism, rivalling the Taliban destruction of the great Buddha of Bamiyan.

There are tens of thousands of less prominent detainees. The story of one Uyghur woman, Gulbahar Haitiwaji, illustrates what must have been the experience of many. Her 2022 book, *How I Survived a Chinese 'Re-education' Camp*, is remarkable, not only for the detail she provides of daily life in the camps, but for the calm and unsensational way in which she recounts her horrific and unjustified incarceration. She describes brutal military-style physical training, parading in serried ranks facing a portrait of Xi Jinping, 'moon face and paternalistic smile against an azure blue background. You'd think we were in Tiananmen Square.' She wanted to scream at him that 'his system would never break' her.

As she was moved from one type of camp to another, she experienced a regime that was a combination of prison and military. Sometimes shackled, always isolated from the outside world and forbidden even to speak their own Uyghur language, the inmates had to pledge their loyalty to China and its leadership. Classes began with, 'Thank you to our great country. Thank you to our Party. Thank you to our dear President Xi Jinping.' And ended with, 'I wish good health to Xi Jinping. Long live President Xi Jinping.' This is reminiscent of the personal adulation of Mao during the Cultural Revolution rather than the Party as a whole, but does indicate, if there were any doubt, that the camps are run according to Xi's instructions.

Accused of unpatriotic behaviour connected with household residence permits and the activities of her family abroad, she was sentenced at a farcical trial to seven years in another re-education centre where she was interrogated and humiliated constantly. After pressure from her family and intervention by French diplomats, she was arbitrarily released and allowed to join her family in Europe. Many Uyghurs and Kazakhs may have had far worse experiences, but Gulbahar's powerful narrative reveals the brutal and often farcical nature of the camp regimes.

How far has Xi Jinping been involved in this unprecedented repression? He has remained behind the scenes and the blame lies with Chen Quanguo, the originator of the camp system. There is, however, no doubt that nothing on this scale could have happened without Xi's knowledge and orders. Leaked documents in what have become known as the 'Xinjiang files' show clearly how Xi formulated the policy in internal speeches, not reported by the Chinese media. He is said to have used words like 'virus' and 'addictive drug' to describe Islamic extremism and prescribed 'a period of painful interventionary treatment'. He referred to the inmates of the internment camps as criminals and called for educational remoulding to continue even after they were released from the camps. This indicates that high-level surveillance was going to continue in Xinjiang. Xi and the CCP feared that conflict in Afghanistan and even Syria could spread to Xinjiang and were determined to prevent what they described as the 'contagion'.

In July 2022 Xi Jinping made a rare and much publicised visit to Xinjiang. He was photographed with a crowd of smiling and clapping people, many in traditional Uyghur dress. He made a point of meeting leaders of the Xinjiang Production and Construction Corps, known as the Bingtuan, which has a crucial role in ensuring PRC control over Xinjiang.

Xi's previous visit had been in 2014. Speaking as he concluded that visit, just after a bomb attack on

Urumqi railway station had killed 79 people, he insisted, 'The battle to combat violence and terrorism will not allow even a moment of slackness, and decisive actions must be taken to resolutely suppress the terrorists' rampant momentum.' He was later reported to have added that China would deal a crushing blow to terrorists and deploy a '"strike-first" strategy'. He reiterated the standard CCP position on Xinjiang, that its long-term stability was vital to the development of the whole of China and its 'unity, ethnic harmony and national security'.

Xi Jinping was not responsible for initiating the repression in Xinjiang: it had been going on for many years before he came to power. He did, however, order its intensification and is directly responsible for the impact on the Uyghur people and their society of the mass incarceration. His policies have resulted in untold damage to the social and religious networks in Xinjiang, but also to the urban and rural economies as many of the key workers have been removed. Xinjiang remains closed to most journalists, academics and other independent observers. We may not know just how much damage has been done until there is a major change of regime in China and credible and reliable evidence is available.

Chapter 11: Xi Jinping Confronts the West

China is now ready to gradually erode American leadership and promote Chinese governance.
Zhao Tong, Financial Times, *March 2023*

CHINA'S RELATIONS WITH THE West – the US, its allies and Europe, broadly speaking – have always been complicated and often difficult. Looking back, the era of Jiang Zemin and Hu Jintao (up to 2012) was a mini golden age: China was open to business, tourism and academic exchanges, and diplomatic relations were actually diplomatic. At the beginning of the Xi Jinping administration there was little change, but relations with the West have deteriorated. Tensions between Beijing and the United States, which were never far below the surface, have reached an alarming level. At the same time, Beijing has attempted to maintain and improve good relations with Western Europe, an important trading partner. These relations were severely tested when

Putin invaded Ukraine in February 2022 (which we will look at in chapter 12).

Xi Jinping has turned to the Global South: this is partly to balance what he sees as an increasingly monopolar global order led by the US but follows on naturally from Xi's signature international investment programme, the Belt and Road initiative, where immense sums have been invested in developing countries. Projects include the China–Pakistan Economic Corridor, a railway in Laos and the Eastern Industrial Zone for manufacturing in a town near Addis Ababa in Ethiopia. The intention is that investing in infrastructure abroad will result in sympathetic allies.

This is not a new strategy: it harks back to the Bandung period of the 1950s and 60s under premier and foreign minister Zhou Enlai, the man who spent much of his career trying to moderate Mao Zedong's most unrealistic policies. China saw itself as part of the economically developing Global South. To some extent, that is still how China sees itself, although it is well on its way to being the single largest economy in the world. But cultural sympathies with developing economies remain and these are increasingly important as relations with the United States and possibly with Russia deteriorate further.

As we have seen, Xi Jinping's political priorities have been primarily domestic: corruption in the Communist Party and government, and poverty alleviation. He has never shown a great interest in international relations. However, addressing the Communist Party Congress in October 2022, he set out his formal position: 'China's international influence, appeal and power to shape the world has significantly increased . . . Confronted with drastic changes in the international landscape, we have maintained firm strategic resolve and shown a fighting spirit.'

On the whole, Xi has left international relations to his foreign minister who from 2013 to 2022 was Wang Yi, a cultivated and well-educated man who, among other things, is said to speak fluent English and Japanese. Wang Yi stepped down as foreign minister in 2022 but became Director of the Central Foreign Affairs Commission Office. As that is a Party rather than a government body, Wang Yi has therefore become the most senior foreign affairs official in China, ranking higher than his replacement as foreign minister, the pugnacious and chauvinistic Qin Gang.

Wang has promoted China's policy of 'principled neutrality', rejecting the idea that Beijing is isolating itself from the international community. Speaking at the Munich Security Conference in

February 2023, he insisted that China 'adopts a responsible attitude towards international disputes and plays a constructive role in accordance with the merits of the matter itself'. Wang and Xi have desperately tried to avoid taking sides on the Russian invasion of Ukraine and 'principled neutrality' is the cover for this.

Xi Jinping might model himself on Mao Zedong in many ways but unlike Mao he has travelled abroad. To be strictly accurate, Mao travelled abroad twice to Moscow to meet Stalin and other senior party officials. He did not like Russia, and they did not like him. It was a bit of a diplomatic disaster, and Zhou Enlai had to be sent for to smooth ruffled feathers. Mao mostly stayed at home after that.

Xi Jinping has been more successful in his international travels. He has visited the United States among other countries, spending some two weeks in Iowa in 1985 as part of an agricultural delegation. His American hosts noted that he 'hardly mentioned his family at all and did not appear to have an enquiring mind'.

When Xi was vice premier, he met President George W. Bush, and in 2013 he had an informal meeting with President Obama. This is the only mention of the United States in any detail in Xi's 2014 book, *The Governance of China*, which in general sets out the official position on his policies. He said, 'I told President Obama explicitly that China will unswervingly follow the path of peaceful development, further its reform and opening up, strive to realise the Chinese dream of the rejuvenation of the Chinese nation and promote the noble cause of peace and development of mankind.'

Xi Jinping went on to express his confidence about the 'new model; of a relationship between major countries such as China and the USA'. He acknowledged that this model was unprecedented but was sure that it would be 'faithfully carried out by the two sides'. He ended the speech by saying, 'the two sides should eschew mistrust and engage in co-operation so as to make cybersecurity a new bright spot in China–U.S. co-operation.' That sounded very positive but unfortunately it was then downhill all the way.

Joe Biden, as vice president to Barack Obama, spent many hours with Xi Jinping, who was his Chinese counterpart at the time. Biden calculated that he travelled 17,000 miles with Xi in China, the rest of Asia and the US, and spent at least 24 hours alone in conversation accompanied only by their personal interpreters. Later, in response to reporters' questions, Biden would say that he knew Xi very well but that he did not consider him a friend. There is a difference in Chinese usage between an 'old friend' (老朋友 *lao pengyou*), someone you have known and dealt with for a long time but who is not necessarily a friend, and a 'good friend' (好朋友 *hao pengyou*) in the English-language sense. Xi has called Biden a *lao pengyou* but has not spoken in public about his opinion of Joe Biden and his administration.

Xi's visits to the United States have strengthened his commitment to the China Dream, in particular the desire to catch up with, or even surpass, the economic development of the United States. This echoes Mao's determination in 1958 to catch up with or surpass the United Kingdom in its steel production and other economic developments. At the time, the UK was hailed as the gold standard of economic development; that is now no more than a distant memory.

Sino–American relations became genuinely problematic during the presidency of Donald Trump between 2017 and 2021. According to Trump, 'Our relationship with China has now probably never, ever been better.' He insisted that he and Xi Jinping had a good and close relationship. 'He's for China, I'm for the US, but other than that, we love each other.' Given the style of Trump's administration, it is hardly surprising that the relationship became chaotic and that the Chinese had no idea what really constituted US policy. The United States under Trump promised deals that could never really be sustained while at the same time threatening and then imposing high tariffs, a particular obsession of Donald Trump. By the time the Trump administration was moving towards its close, high and even punitive tariffs were being imposed by the United States and, not surprisingly, Beijing initiated counter measures.

The diplomatic difficulties were illustrated by the case of the Huawei company, which makes mobile phones but also a great deal of security and other electronic equipment. Initially, the Huawei dispute between America and China was on two fronts. Firstly, the chief financial officer of Huawei, Meng Wanzhou, was detained in Canada and the United States issued extradition warrants as they wished to try her in the United States on charges of fraud and conspiracy to commit fraud. The case against her was connected with allegations that Huawei was trying to avoid international sanctions against Iran. As the Huawei case unfolded, concerns were raised about possible security risks associated with using Huawei and similar electronic equipment in Western security systems. Some argued that Huawei software could assist surveillance by Chinese security organisations.

In June 2019, President Trump met Xi Jinping in Osaka in Japan, reversed his position on Huawei and reduced the tariffs. Xi by this time had become exasperated by the flip-flopping of United States policy, the inconsistency, and the utter confusion of international relations under the Trump administration. In spite of that, it became possible in January 2020 for a trade deal to be signed between China and the United States. It was called 'phase one' of a trade deal, which indicates that it was far from being a settled treaty, but it was signed when Liu He, vice president and Politburo member and close confidant of Xi Jinping, met Trump in the White House. Rather than it being a genuine trade deal – and Trump always claimed to be 'master of the deal' – it has often been described as merely a truce in the trade war.

2020 of course saw the arrival of Covid, with the devastating effect that it had on international trade and travel. International priorities were switched from trade and diplomacy to health. Chinese diplomacy moved from being pragmatic, calm and thoughtful to what became known as 'wolf warrior' diplomacy. This rather fanciful name took its name from a film, 战狼 *Zhanlang*, which is more literally translated as *War Wolf*. At the centre of the plot is a PLA Special Forces Unit in an operation against smugglers and foreign mercenaries close to China's southern border. This film and its successor, *Wolf Warrior 2*, struck a chord with nationalistic Chinese and the name has been applied to an aggressive, often vituperative, tone in statements by foreign ministry officials in Beijing when they publicly attacked the United States for what they alleged as its attempts to contain China. It was noticeable that the 'wolf warrior' style of diplomatic rhetoric increased as Xi Jinping campaigned to secure an extension to his decade in office, the assumption being that it would appeal to the hard-line and old-fashioned style of senior Communist Party cadres and the military.

Once the extension of Xi's term of office as Communist Party general secretary was secured, there seemed to be at least a temporary return to more conventional diplomatic exchanges, but even with his reappointment as president in March 2023 there were aggressive speeches by his new foreign minister, Qin Gang. The name 'wolf warrior' might be new, but the style of diplomatic conflict is not. There are echoes of the Cultural Revolution in the 1960s when diplomats and diplomatic language became violent in the extreme. Sometimes the behaviour of diplomats became violent; one was immortalised on film for wielding an axe outside the

Chinese embassy in London and others demonstrated outside Chinese government buildings in Hong Kong.

One of the most surprising outcomes of the transition to Xi's third term was Beijing's role in brokering a deal in April 2023 between the governments of Iran and Saudi Arabia, countries that had been in conflict with each other for decades, particularly over the war in Yemen. It was strange to see China's most senior diplomat, Wang Yi, bringing together the hands of the representatives of the Shi'ite and Sunni states at a press conference in Beijing as China tried to demonstrate its new and influential role in international relations. Relations between Saudi Arabia and Iran had become so tense that for the previous seven years they had not even maintained diplomatic relations, and China's apparent success in guiding them towards a rapprochement will also enhance Beijing's abilities to trade in the Middle East. It throws out a challenge to the United States, which previously would have seen itself as the only honest broker in Middle Eastern relations.

Wang Yi and the man who was to succeed him as foreign minister, Qin Wang, shared the limelight but it later transpired that the initiative for the mediation came directly from Xi Jinping. In an interview for *People's Daily*, the CCP's official newspaper, the head of the foreign ministry's Middle East department revealed that the idea was broached during Xi Jinping's state visit to Saudi Arabia in December 2022 and then raised with the Iranian President Ebrahim Raisi when he visited Beijing the following February. China's intervention in the Middle East was unprecedented but Xi Jinping indicated that he intended to offer Beijing's services as a neutral mediator in other conflicts in the region. Xi's spokesman made it clear that these initiatives were deliberately designed to counter US influence in the Middle East.

This Iran-Saudi deal marked the beginning of a new and more assertive role for China in international affairs. Xi clearly believes that the decline of the US is inevitable and that the time has come for Beijing to take the lead in establishing a new world order. This was evident in his state visit to Moscow in March 2023 and reiterated when he met political leaders from Europe the following month. To achieve his foreign policy goals, Xi has centralised and taken personal control of both foreign and defence policy. He has control over not only the Central Military Commission but also the National Security Council and the Central Committee Leading Groups that are responsible for international affairs and security. On Sino–Russian relations especially, his personal involvement is evident. Xi can use this authority to impose his own foreign policy without having to balance hawks and doves in his administration.

Europe is important to Beijing. It is an important trading partner and also useful to counterbalance the power of the US. The French president, Emmanuel Macron, completed his state visit to China by taking tea with Xi Jinping in Guangzhou, one of the key drivers of China's economic development, and incidentally where Xi's father, Xi Zhongxun, had been party secretary in the 1980s. Ursula von der Leyen, president of the European Commission, joined Macron for some of the meetings but had separate meetings with Xi Jinping and other officials, which were covered in the Chinese media more than in the West. Both European leaders pressed Xi to use his leverage on Putin to end the war in Ukraine. Subsequent informal comments by President Macron were interpreted as a willingness by France to take a less confrontational approach over the war. Some Western commentators insisted that Macron was pushing French interests ahead of European ones, but in a prominent op-ed for the *Financial Times* on 12 April 2023 he argued strongly for 'European sovereignty'. There was no indication from Xi Jinping that these requests for intervention would influence him, but that was only to be expected. Any overtures to Putin would be strictly private.

In April 2023 the Chinese ambassador to France, Lu Shaye, a diplomat who flaunts his 'wolf warrior' credentials, horrified European governments by asserting that ex-Soviet territories such as Lithuania, Latvia and Estonia, which became independent states after the collapse of the Soviet Union, had no 'effective status' under international law. He either misunderstood completely the transformation of Russia's post-Soviet relations with the Baltic States and Eastern Europe or he was echoing the Putin fantasy of reincorporating these territories into a 'greater Russia'. This was not helpful to Xi Jinping's proposal that China should lead a peace initiative to end the war in Ukraine.

In an extraordinary reversal, his statement was retracted and contradicted by the official spokesperson of the Chinese foreign ministry, Mao Ying. She reports to the foreign minister, Qin Gang, himself given to 'wolf warrior diplomacy'. This confusion within the ministry is evidence of a power struggle as career diplomats manoeuvre to avoid belligerent outbursts. The U-turn may have been on Xi Jinping's orders: he has not commented on his ambassador's alarming assertions or the reversal, but then he never does. He remains aloof and will never be inter-viewed by the foreign media, but outbursts like this does raise questions about how far he controls the foreign ministry.

Chapter 12: Xi and Putin: Friends Without Limit?

> Only Xi can offer a warm handshake to Putin in
> public – and a twisted arm in private.
> *Gideon Rachman*, Financial Times,
> *May 2023*

THE RELATIONSHIP BETWEEN XI Jinping and
Vladimir Putin has been one of the greatest enigmas
of Xi's administration. Contemporary commentators often oversimplify China–Russia relations by
reducing them to personal relations between Xi Jinping and Vladimir Putin. Some treat them as if they
were almost identical, a tsar and an emperor, or at
least as if they had identical roles.

But there is more to it than that. China's relations with Russia and the former USSR have always
been complicated. This is partly for geographical
reasons; they share a long border that extends for over
2,600 miles. The complexity also results from the
asymmetric development of their revolutions in the
twentieth century and the collapse of communism

in the USSR while the CCP remains in power in China.

When Vladimir Putin travelled to Beijing on 4 February 2022 to attend the opening of the Winter Olympic Games, there was almost universal aston-ishment at the wording of a statement issued jointly with Xi Jinping on relations between the two states. It was going to be a 'no limits' partnership with no forbidden zones. Sceptics wondered how real this was or how long it would last, but few could have known that, within 20 days, Russia would have invaded Ukraine. Not only did Putin fail to consult China about the wisdom of his 'special operation', he did not even warn his supposed close ally Xi that he was going to invade – a strange interpretation of a 'no limits' partnership. This was deeply embarrass-ing for Xi, so naturally there is no mention of this in official statements. Off-the-record comments by Chinese diplomats have insisted that this phrase was really only rhetoric.

Since the invasion, the relationship between Moscow and Beijing has come under severe strain. International attention has focused on the question of whether China would support Russia's invasion of Ukraine, in particular whether it would supply lethal weapons or other materials to Russia to assist it in its prosecution of the war. Perhaps not surprisingly, the phrase 'no limits' comes up less and less in communications by the Chinese.

There is a long history of Russia-Chinese tensions, misunderstandings and diplomatic duplicity which goes back to the eastern expansion of the Tsarist empire in the eighteenth and nineteenth centuries and the westward expansion of the Manchu Qing dynasty's Chinese Empire at roughly the same time. It was the convergence of these imperial expansions that created the modern Sino–Russian border. Although the Russians and Chinese have attempted to create a modern diplomacy, and modern political and economic relations, a legacy of mistrust remains. Part of that mistrust involves border disputes, some of which were not resolved until the early twenty-first century.

When the Chinese Communist Party came to power in 1949, the USSR saw itself as the communist 'elder brother'. Mao Zedong did not relish being the 'younger brother', particularly after the death of Stalin in 1953, and relations deteriorated. By 1960, relations had worsened and technical advisers from the Soviet bloc were withdrawn. Military activity on the border between China and Russia escalated and bloody infantry and tank battles were fought there in 1969.

Relations between China and the Soviet Union – and then Russia – never really recovered. In 1991, the USSR itself collapsed and Sino–Soviet relations were replaced by complex international negotiations with the Russian Federation and new Central Asian regimes such as Kazakhstan, Kyrgyzstan and Tajikistan. Mutual distrust remained, but China and Russia maintained common cause against what they saw as an emerging global order entirely dominated by the United States and its Western allies.

Relations between Xi Jinping and Vladimir Putin were believed to be good after Xi came to power in 2012. However, films of their meetings show only formal occasions, and neither side comments on the other in personal terms, so it is difficult to assess what the two leaders think of each other. Xi Jinping made a state visit to Moscow in 2013 and has repeated that every two years. Putin reciprocated and made his own state visit to Beijing in 2018. What to some had seemed a marriage of convenience with no real community of interest had evolved into a long-term strategic partnership. Putin and Xi have met dozens of times and Xi refers to him as a 'dear friend' (亲爱的朋友 *qin'ai de pengyou*), which is rather different from the 'old friend' (老朋友 *lao pengyou*) used for Joe Biden. Since Putin's invasion of Ukraine, which he neglected to warn Xi about, this apparent closeness has come under great stress.

Xi Jinping set out his formal thoughts on Russia at the Moscow State Institute of International Relations in March 2013. Surveying the complex international world order, he confirmed his views that 'China and Russia enjoy a high degree of complementarity in development strategy' and that a 'strong and prosperous Russia' was in China's interests. In Xi's view, 'the relationship between China and Russia [was] one of the most important bilateral relations in the world' and 'the best relationship between major countries'. He strongly endorsed Putin's view that 'Russia needs a prosperous and stable China, and China needs a strong and successful Russia'.

Xi Jinping is in an increasingly difficult position, attempting a risky balancing act. He does not want to alienate his European counterparts, who are almost all completely in favour of Ukraine's resistance to Russia's invasion. Nor does he want to alienate the Global South where there is less interest in European wars. As his predecessors did in the 1950s, Xi sees the developing countries of the Global South as an important locus for alternative action against dominant Western powers. He is trying to avoid committing himself to supporting the Russian invasion while claiming that China still has a close relationship with Russia. Below the surface there will have been great anger at the position Putin has

put Xi in. Xi Jinping cannot ignore China's relationship with its Russian neighbour. Statements from
the Chinese Ministry of Foreign Affairs have been
careful to avoid giving overt support for Putin's war
in Ukraine. Many Western leaders hope that Beijing
will act as a restraint on Putin, especially that Beijing will be able to persuade him not to deploy
nuclear weapons, even battlefield nuclear weapons
with their limited range. Xi is the one political leader
who could exert some pressure on Putin and his
actions in Ukraine. If he is doing that, there is little
evidence to date of any change; in fact, there was a
revival of the aggressive and rather crude 'wolf-
warrior' diplomacy from the new minister of foreign
affairs, Qin Gang.

This did not last long and Qin Gang himself
disappeared from view for several weeks before
being removed from his post in July 2023. There
were reports that his dismissal was decided at a previously unscheduled meeting of the NPC Standing
Committee and was surrounded by confusion. No
reasons were given, and Qin's name was removed
from published documents and then reinstated.
Wang Yi, his predecessor, was reappointed foreign
minister in an unusual move.

When Xi Jinping's planned state visit to Moscow
in March 2023 was announced, there was immediate

speculation that this would demonstrate how tight China–Russia ties were – especially as Putin had just been served with a warrant alleging war crimes by the International Criminal Court. Xi arrived in Moscow on 21 March armed with a 12-point plan for achieving peace in Ukraine, *China's Position on the Political Settlement of the Ukraine Crisis,* which would have effectively legitimised Moscow's invasion and annexation. Xi and Putin addressed each other as 'dear friend' and together strove to create the impression of a solid united front. Xi presented himself as a potential honest broker and peacemaker and the question of Russian demands for weaponry that could be used in Ukraine was not mentioned. A joint statement expressed approval of Beijing's 'positive role' and 'objective unbiased position' on the Ukraine war but there were no announcements of agreements on economic aid to Russia, including the Power of Siberia 2 pipeline (PS2), which would supply Russian gas to China via Mongolia. By the end of May 2023, Beijing had still not committed fully to the project. A press conference at the end of Xi's March visit was illuminating. Putin gave a long and rambling list of all the benefits of a close alliance with China. Xi's response was formal, vague and brief; it concluded abruptly. What emerged from the meeting was that, below the superficial diplomatic niceties, the 'no limits' agreement was far from being an agreement between equal states. Russia was increasingly dependent on China, and this gave Beijing leverage. Whether and how it will exercise this leverage remains to be seen.

Eight days after Lu Shaye's alarming statement on the standing of post-Soviet states, and in a move that can only be described as damage control, Xi Jinping telephoned Volodymyr Zelenskyy, the Ukrainian president. Zelenskyy had been asking for this contact for many weeks and Chinese sources insisted the timing was coincidental. In a call that lasted for an hour, Xi Jinping offered to send a special envoy, former ambassador to Moscow, Liu Hui, to shuttle between Moscow and Kyiv. Xi's contact with Zelenskyy is an attempt show that China is not simply pro-Russia, but in the absence of concrete actions, Xi will be accused of playing both sides against the middle.

When the possibility of Xi mediating between Russia and Ukraine was first raised, it was considered laughable. This was gradually replaced with scepticism and by early May, Gideon Rachman, the *Financial Times*'s respected international relations analyst, was concluding that only Beijing might have levers that could force Putin to make meaningful concessions that might be accepted by Kyiv.

The future of Sino–Soviet relations is unpredictable but it is likely that the alliance with Moscow will continue to be a high priority in the light of what Beijing confidently sees as the inevitable decline of the US-led West and the rise of the East led by China – 'the east wind prevailing over the west wind', as Mao Zedong put it decades previously – but it is increasingly an alliance dominated by China.

Chapter 13: President for Life?

He has consolidated so much power and now put
in place a new team made up of his trusted men.
Going forward, his team will be the one
that is accountable.

Alfred Wu, South China Morning Post, *March 2023*

AND NOW WE RETURN to Xi Jinping's extended term
of office. This extension might seem to confirm support for his hard-line stance (all 2,952 members
present endorsed Xi), but the near unanimity of the
confirmation vote reflects deference to party unity
rather than loyalty to Xi personally. He has not publicly made his intentions clear as to whether this
next five years will be his last in power, or if not,
how much longer he is really planning to stay. Since
the confirmation, his approach seems to have soft-
ened: this could be simply because he has achieved
his short-term goal or that he has made a deal with
more moderate groups in the party hierarchy.

At the National People's Congress, Xi introduced his new team. Premier Li Keqiang, who had served, albeit ineffectually, throughout Xi's first decade, stood down and was replaced by Li Qiang. He is regarded as a staunch Xi Jinping loyalist, but he is also seen as more friendly to business and finance than many of his colleagues. Since Xi's previous few years were marked by attacks on business, particularly large internet enterprises, this is an interesting development. As party leader in Shanghai, Li Qiang met Elon Musk in 2018 and persuaded him to build Musk's first overseas car factory in China. Li also served as governor of Zhejiang province and party secretary of Jiangsu province; he knows the whole Yangtze Delta Economic Region well and was also on unusually good terms with some of the best-known business names in China, particularly Jack Ma (Ma Yun), owner of Alibaba.

Li Qiang was also behind the development to expand Shanghai's stock market by including a Nasdaq-style tech sector market. Some analysts had predicted that Xi Jinping would replace all the officials at the head of the finance ministries and elsewhere in the finance sector. In the end there was some surprise at how little change there had been. Yi Gang, the governor of the People's Bank of China, China's central bank, retained his post, as did the existing finance and commerce ministers. One new appointment was another Xi loyalist, He Lifeng, as a vice premier. He Lifeng is a professional economist and finance specialist whose previous jobs included overseeing the National Development and Reform Commission, China's principal central planning agency. More importantly, he was well known to Xi Jinping as he had worked in Xiamen and other parts of Fujian province during Xi's time there.

These moves leave a solid core of technocrats at the heart of China's financial system, but Xi made it clear that he was going to put some of the regulatory functions of the People's Bank of China under the control of a new State Financial Regulatory Commission, which he would chair. This gives Xi and his loyalists ultimate control of the finance sector but also allows for technical expertise and continuity in the leadership of the banks and the ministries.

Xi compromised by keeping some of the existing officials in place but was not prepared to relinquish overall control. By the evening of Thursday 16 March 2023, the precise way in which he proposed to exercise control over China's financial bodies became clearer. State media announced a list of new Communist Party committees to oversee government ministries and regulators that are already under the control of the State Council, China's cabinet.

A Central Technology Committee will direct science and technology research and development and most importantly integrate civilian and military projects. Other new bodies include a Central Finance Committee and a revamped Central Financial Work Committee, which is designed to 'reinforce the Party's political and ideological work in the financial system'. Control over Hong Kong is also being brought more directly under Xi's authority rather than that of the State Council as previously, although in this case the existing body is reorganised as a party body rather than a government one.

These compromises and attempts to resolve them reveal internal party and government tensions on the economy and finance. These conflicts will be thrashed out and probably resolved in relations between the technocratic government bodies and Xi's political supervisory bodies. The outcome will depend on Xi's ability to continue to insist on his own way against more rational voices in his new five-year term. The dynamics of the Xi Jinping–Li Qiang relationship will be crucial.

Xi clearly lost support among the captains of industry in the last five years of his tenure. This was especially so in the hi-tech sectors and any enterprises that require foreign capital, expertise or cooperation. The long-term effect of detaining or restricting the

activities of high-profile individuals such as Jack
Ma, the Alibaba CEO, cannot be calculated precisely,
but there is no doubt that business leaders would
prefer a leader who is more genuinely friendly to
business. Li Qiang may be that person; Xi Jinping is
not. Jack Ma's reappearance has been taken by some
entrepreneurs as a sign that Xi Jinping's harsh regulatory crackdown on businesses is being relaxed. If
so, this will be a relief to China's wealthiest whose
assets have also been hit by Xi's zero-Covid policies
and the collapse of the property market. Jack Ma has
spoken of business leaders having to 'walk on ice'
during Xi's regulatory crackdown, especially those
who ran internet companies. It was bad enough for
small companies, he said, but the bigger they were,
the harder it was to deal with the government.

How much support does Xi have among the
population in general? In a society in which to differ
can be treated as dissent, and dissent suggests
treachery, it is extremely difficult to say. There are
straws in the wind. The popularity of Winnie-the-
Pooh internet memes and other satirical comments
indicates a profound dissatisfaction among the young
and better educated. For many people though, Xi
is admired for standing up for China in his foreign policy and for his determination to eradicate
corruption.

In spite of the overwhelming pressure to conform, there have been criticisms of Xi Jinping, often from those who have left, but also those working inside China. In an interview for an article by Mercy Kuo in *The Diplomat*, Feng Chongyi of the University of Technology in Sydney is scathing about the attempts to create a 'Xi Jinping Thought on Socialism with Chinese Characteristics for a New Era'. He described it as a 'mixture of dissimilar ingredients taken from his predecessors [reinforced] with the old fancy slogans of the past including the slogans of Maoist China and reforming China'. Feng had been barred from leaving China because of his views on human rights but managed to leave in April 2017. While few would oppose Xi's campaign against corruption, there were many who insisted that it avoids the real problems. For Zhang Yuxin, working in a Washington think tank, Asia Policy Point, and writing for *The Diplomat* in August 2014, 'Xi's anticorruption campaign overlooks the core of the problem. There is a gap between rich and poor but he should have focused more on the latter . . . To win full legitimacy, Xi needs to go beyond removing high-level officials and devote more attention to domestic policies and political reforms.'

Dingding Chen, based at Jinan University in Guangzhou, is more supportive of Xi's leadership and his China Dream. Writing in 2014 for *The Diplomat*, he asserted that 'Xi and his colleagues are determined to find a suitable road for China which cannot be separated from China's unique history and national conditions.' For Chen, Xi is a 'visionary leader', who 'clearly sees where China should be in the future'. Xi 'enjoys a high level of legitimacy among elites as well as the masses', 'knows how to play the right strategies'; and has 'the ability to prioritise tasks and balance between different groups and demands'. While the first part of Chen's assessment is vague and ingratiating, the remainder rings true and lends support to the idea of Xi as a politician in the Song Jiang mode.

Xi's credibility was severely damaged when he was obliged, under pressure from the Chinese people, to end the Covid lockdown policy so suddenly in December 2022: it showed weakness, when strength had been his major selling point. Over 120,000 Chinese people died from Covid according to the World Health Organisation, but some analysts insist that the number is much higher. The severity of the lockdowns in Shanghai and other large cities triggered unprecedented mass demonstrations against Xi and local party officials. Although the official Chinese position was that the end of the lockdowns was possible because of a change in the virus, nobody was fooled.

The bizarre and unprecedented manner in which Xi treated former President Hu Jintao, his one-time mentor, by ejecting him so publicly from the 20th Party Congress in October 2022, raised questions about Xi's control of the party and the level of opposition from supporters of Hu, mostly considered to be part of the Youth League faction. The more efficient management of the National People's Congress has to some extent mitigated the damage done at the Party Congress, but that crude misstep will not be forgotten.

Xi has an extra five years, not another ten, which had been the rule when he was appointed in 2012. There are no indications that he has nominated a successor, even informally, but there are plenty of claimants waiting in the wings. Could new premier, Li Qiang, be among them? Time is running out for Xi Jinping; he is 70 and has already broken the rules of succession inside the CCP. He must either plan on a further extension or decide how to bow out and leave his mission to someone he can trust to follow in his footsteps. There are few signs that he is weakening, either in his personal fitness or his hold on power. His public humiliation of Hu Jintao was so extraordinary that it indicates a serious miscalculation. Did he for some reason allow his personal feelings to override his political judgement?

To date there has been no indication of a possible successor. That can only mean bitter and desperate, but largely invisible, power struggles within the party until a successor emerges.

Some Western analysts – and all those who identify as 'China hawks' – insist that Xi Jinping is a threat to the West. Conflict with Xi Jinping's China does pose a serious threat to Western security, particularly the possibility of a military conflict with the United States and its allies in the Pacific, but only a one-sided analysis can assert that blame would rest solely with the Chinese side. There are many potential flashpoints that could lead to such a war, including the Koreas and the South China Sea, but an attempt by Beijing to incorporate Taiwan into the PRC by force, or a declaration of sovereignty and independence by Taiwan, would inevitably trigger such a conflict.

As I have already noted, the Pacific War of 1941 to 1945 was immensely costly in lives and resources. It devastated the nations, large and small, that became involved directly or indirectly and triggered political and social change on an unprecedented scale. It put an end to the rule of the old colonial powers of Britain and the Netherlands. That might have been a desirable outcome for the colonial subjects of those powers, but the cost was horrific and avoiding a repeat of that war must be the highest priority for all involved in international relations in the Asia-Pacific region.

We should also stand back and ask ourselves whether the West poses a threat to China. Western politicians and diplomats will argue that they are not threatening China with a military assault. This is true, but the West is attempting to contain the rise of China, especially in the South China Sea, arguing with justification that it is protecting internationally agreed sea lanes and borders. China, like Russia, *perceives* that it is under threat. Governments, like individuals, act on the basis of how they perceive the situation, not on what other actors see as the reality.

The West, and particularly the US, tend to see China's current position as a threat to what had become more or less a monopolar world, dominated by the US after the collapse of the USSR. There is a better way of looking at the situation. China's economic status and international influence are rising and competition for economic and political influence is inevitable. The diplomatic challenge for the international community during the rest of the twenty-first century is to manage this competition in a way that avoids military conflict. China should be included in that 'international community'. Meeting the challenge might be more difficult as Xi Jinping remains in power, but his intentions are uncertain. He is given to tough statements complaining about the West's 'all-round containment, encirclement and suppression', but his trade representatives have resumed contacts – he is due to visit San Francisco for the 31st Asia-Pacific Economic Cooperation intergovernment forum in November 2023 and diplomatic links at all levels are improving. We have no idea whether a successor will be more or less belligerent, but we can be sure that whoever it is will insist on putting China's interests first. Xi will be a difficult act to follow.

Afterword

It is one year since the 20th Congress in October 2022 that confirmed Xi Jinping's additional five-year term as general secretary of the Chinese Communist Party and paved the way for the extension of his term of office as president from March 2023. Xi's position still appears to be unchallenged but his unexpected absence from high-profile international meetings has raised eyebrows, as have the sudden and unexplained disappearances of a number of senior officials.

The sudden dismissal of Qin Gang as foreign minister has never been explained officially but rumours have circulated about an affair with a media personality and a surrogate pregnancy – which certainly would not have been acceptable to the puritanical Xi Jinping. An unscheduled meeting of the National People's Congress Standing Committee was convened to dismiss Qin and replace him with his predecessor Wang Yi, who had been promoted to be his superior in a CCP body. These were unusual moves which suggest a hasty decision.

Senior military officers in the PLA Rocket Force resigned after investigations into procurement irregularities but the disappearance and presumed dismissal of Li Shangfu, the minister of defence, was more consequential. His removal has not been confirmed so far, but reports also link him to corruption in procurement.

At the August 2023 BRICs summit meeting in Johannesburg, Xi Jinping did not attend a business forum he had been expected to address; his speech was given by the minister for commerce, Wang Wentao. Xi did, however, appear at the conference, where he was presented with the Order of South Africa by President Cyril Ramaphosa.

Of greater significance was Xi's failure to attend the G20 meeting in New Delhi in September 2023. Many analysts concluded that this was a political and diplomatic absence, engineered as a deliberate snub to India's prime minister Narendra Modi. Clashes in Aksai Chin, on the border between China and India, in 2020 and 2021 had left troops dead on both sides. China views India as a serious competitor for leadership of the Global South, so this explanation for Xi's absence is credible.

At the G20 meeting, Li Qiang, the Chinese premier and a close ally of Xi, deputised for his chief, taking great pains to demonstrate that he did not

have the same status as Xi, for example, not travelling in the special aircraft that Xi would have used,
had he attended. In spite of these careful optics, Li
Qiang's profile has been raised internationally and
he was sometimes referred to as 'China's No.2',
although this is not accurate in terms of the CCP
pecking order. Xi also failed to attend the Eastern
Economic Forum, hosted by Vladimir Putin, in
Vladivostok on 12 September. On that occasion
Zhang Guoqing, a deputy premier, attended in his
place.

The unexplained dismissals of Qin Gang and Li
Shangfu suggest that there has been serious conflict
and confusion within the foreign relations and defence
establishment in Beijing. It is, therefore, just as likely
that Xi decided to remain in Beijing on those occasions so as not to lose control of the situation. He is
scheduled to attend the Asia-Pacific Economic
Cooperation Leaders' Week in San Francisco in
November 2023. If he does not attend that meeting,
speculation about his position will inevitably increase.
A statement issued in the name of the Ministry of
State Security (MSS) on 4 September appeared to
suggest that Xi's participation in the meeting was
dependent on the USA showing 'enough sincerity' in
diplomatic relations. The fact that this statement
came from the ministry responsible for China's

overseas intelligence agency, rather than from the Ministry of Foreign Affairs, which would have been the normal channel, has prompted speculation that Xi was using the MSS to control divisions of opinion within the diplomatic establishment.

The institutionalisation of Xi's personal philosophy – Xi Jinping Thought – continues throughout Chinese society. The *Financial Times* reported in September 2023 on a new textbook that had been published for first-year university students, *College English for New Era*, that includes many quotations from speeches and articles written by Xi himself. In order to 'incorporate national consciousness into foreign language education', 'help students build confidence in Chinese culture' and 'tell a good China story', it emphasises Chinese achievements, including the reception of the 2022 Winter Olympics in Beijing: a planned new edition is likely to contain extracts from Xi Jinping's speech to the 20th Party Congress that extended his term of office. This contrasts with the previous generation of textbooks that introduced aspects of Western culture to Chinese students.

At the time of writing, there is no official indication as to what will happen when the agreed five-year extension of Xi's positions expires. He shows no sign of agreeing to retire quietly: pessimistic analysts predict that he intends to remain in power for many more years, but he has formidable opponents and rivals within the senior ranks of the CCP who are intent on preventing this from happening. We will have to watch as the drama unfolds, even though most of it will be behind closed doors.

Michael Dillon
October 2023

Acknowledgements

I am indebted to a great many individuals and organisations in China for my understanding of the country and its leaders. The individuals are too many to mention and, in the current climate of suspicion and tension, it would not be helpful to name names. I am grateful to many people connected with the Chinese Academy of Social Sciences in Beijing, Shanghai, Jiangxi, Anhui, Gansu, Ningxia and Xinjiang and to colleagues from Tsinghua University, Renmin University of China and Xinjiang University. Outside China, I have benefited from discussions with colleagues from George Washington University, Université Libre de Bruxelles, University of Göttingen, Hong Kong University of Science and Technology and the Lau China Institute at King's College London.

Joyce Dillon typed the manuscript at great speed, Shammah Banerjee has been a perceptive editor whose constructive and critical input has been invaluable, and timely suggestions from Amanda Waters have helped to sharpen the focus of the book.